JIMI

An intimate biography of

Jimi Hendrix

by

Curtis Knight

PRAEGER PUBLISHERS
New York · Washington

Published in the United States of America in 1974
by Praeger Publishers, Inc.
111 Fourth Avenue, New York, N.Y. 10003

Library of Congress Cataloging in Publication Data

Knight, Curtis.
Jimi.

1. Hendrix, Jimi. I. Title.
ML410.H476K6   784'.092'4 [B]   73-9394
ISBN 0-275-19880-4

Printed in the United States of America

*To Jimi and to all musical children
in the world*

Acknowledgements

I would like to thank the following people for their help in the preparation of this book :

James Allen Hendrix, Pete Townshend, Jean Bogart, Eric Burdon, Monika Danneman, Fayne Pridgon, Kathy Etchingham, Devon Wilson, Jan Persson, The Isley Brothers, Mitch Mitchell, John and Yoko Lennon, Miles Davis, Robin Trower, Eddie Kramer, Buddy Miles, Ray Lucas, Joyce the Voice, Mark Paternostro, Noel Redding, Yvette Morgan-Griffiths, John Munday, Leslie Banks, Laurens Van Houten, Marianne Faithfull.

Contents

CHAPTER ONE

The coming of a genius

Jimi Hendrix was a messenger from another world. Genius guitarist, sent from another time and another place, to give us a message of Love, Peace and Freedom. I was fortunate to have known, loved and been associated with him. Perhaps I played a small part in his destiny.

He was born James Marshall Hendrix on 27 November 1942 in Seattle, Washington, a city of half a million people. His father, James Allen Hendrix, was a self-employed gardener and the tools of his trade were a truck, a lawn-mower and assorted hoses and shears for cutting weeds and pruning trees. His living depended heavily on something outside his control and something within it : the weather, and his own proficiency. How well he did his job was vitally important because there were always other gardeners around, engaged in what's called competitive bidding. Stealing customers is what it was.

It was a precarious living for a man as kind and considerate as Jimi Hendrix's father—a man short in stature but filled with love, patience and understanding. And it was matched by a precarious home-life. Jimi's mother was a full-blooded

Cherokee Indian, and had a very different personality from her husband's.

Jimi once said, 'My mother and Dad used to fall out a lot. My Dad was very religious and level-headed, but my mother used to like having a good time, and dressing up. She used to drink a lot, and didn't take care of herself. She died when I was ten, but she was a real groovy mother.'

So at a very early age, Jimi experienced the feelings of a divided home, with his mother away most of the time. The way he saw it, she loved him and enjoyed seeing him whenever she could, but it was impossible for her to be a full-time mother because of circumstances. He told me, 'I was too young to understand what was happening at the time between my mom and dad—I mean, you know: why they weren't grooving together in the same pad—but I realised later, after my mother died, that sometimes if two people can't get it together, well, the next best thing to do is to split.'

These, then, were the parents who gave birth to this 20th Century musical messiah. There was no manger, no wise men bearing gifts; but nevertheless he was destined for greatness.

One of his aunts describes how she remembers him as a baby: 'Jimi was very shy and humble, but with the ability to comprehend all that went on around him.' And as a young boy, he seemed withdrawn and mysterious—very much of an individual, not pursuing the ordinary things that most young boys pursue. He had the courage of his convictions and the ability to stand alone at a very early age. A true Sagittarian.

In appearance, too, he stood out from the others—because, ironically, his hair was unusually short. Asked, at the height of his popularity, why he grew his hair so long, Jimi replied: 'I think maybe I grow it long because when I was young, my dad used to cut my hair like a skinned chicken, and all my friends used to call me Slick Bean.'

One very significant incident, serving to increase Jimi's self-reliance, occurred when he was eight years old. He attended the Dunlan Baptist Church in Seattle every Sunday, and could hardly wait, each week, to hear the music sung by the choir. I remember Jimi saying, 'The music just seemed to engulf me and carry me away with it. It kind of went through me from my head to my feet. I really dug the way that preacher weaved his hypnotic magic spell over the people.' If you've ever been to that kind of church then you know what he is talking about: tambourines beating and feet stomping—even people being saved and talking in unknown tongues—and such happy shoutings and gyrations. Too out of sight to describe. And then, one Sunday, the incident occurred without warning. Jimi explained it to me —sitting looking very perplexed and angry, as though he was reliving it.

'They kicked me out of that Holy Roller church—when I was only eight years old! They said I wasn't dressed properly. Are you ready for that?! I walked out very embarrassed, because the preacher made a real big thing out of it. A grandstand play. And I swore I would never go in that church again as long as I lived.'

But the musical experience he had got from attending church was not the beginning of his musical education. Jimi had only been three or four years old when he had begun to show a distinct interest in music. His father aroused this interest because he played the spoons and comb at home, Jimi told me.

Now the playing of the spoons goes back to the days of slavery in America, when the slaves had virtually no outlets except the spiritual outlet of singing hymns and listening to jack-legged preachers telling them of that brighter day somewhere. But the slaves had an uncanny genius for musical improvisation. They made bass instruments out of the plantation bosses' old hand-me-down tin bath tubs, by putting a hole in the centre of the tub, sticking a stick down into it about four feet high, and tying a string to the stick; holding the string in various positions along the stick with one hand and plucking the string with the other produced amazing assortments of bass-like sounds.

The spoons came out of that same improvisational era. As often as it were possible, the slaves absconded from the big house with some of the silverware, and then certain of the spoons were selected on the basis of age, size and sound compatibility. Then, with the deftness of any instrumental virtuoso, the selected spoons were played while held between two or more fingers—clanked together to produce a variety of different and interesting sounds.

Jimi's father was very good with the spoons, and Jimi at three or four years old turned a curious eye and interested ear in the direction of his father whenever he played them. These and the comb—played, as most people know, by blowing and humming at the same time on a selected kind of wax paper laid across it—were the beginning of Jimi's musical education.

It continued from there, and not long after that preacher threw him out of church, Jimi was finally given a guitar by his uncle—who knew that he was always picking up things like brooms and sticks: any reasonable facsimile of a guitar he could find, pretending to be playing.

The guitar immediately became his whole life, cutting out other things like the unusual ball-game Jimi told me about that had happened after his younger brother Leon came along when Jimi was five. 'I got a whipping,' he told me, 'for kind of bouncing Leon over the floor like a rubber ball.'

With a guitar at last, Jimi spent many hours every day listening to every blues record he could lay his hands on, and he was particularly intrigued by Muddy Waters, Howling

Wolf, Lightning Hopkins, B. B. King, Arthur (Big Boy) Crud-up and Robert Johnson—all southern-born early blues greats.

It is said by members of his family that Jimi showed an unnatural genius for the guitar almost immediately. 'Jimi would hear something on a record and a few minutes later he would be able to play it and improve on it.'

Being left-handed gave him a flair—a stylishness—from the very beginning, and as Jimi continued to learn how to live and how to play in his own way, the guitar became his method of communication.

He was never really into school; the less he saw of it the better he liked it. I remember him saying that 'after I learned how to read and write, I figured there wasn't much more they could tell me, because I was more interested in the next world than this one—because I didn't like very much the way this one is.'

So, uninterruptedly, Jimi's guitar continued to occupy most of his time; and after a while, word started to get around among the kids at school that he was pretty good. He talked to me about one of the fringe benefits of that—one of the bonuses of becoming popular as a musician:

'Girls that had their noses stuck up, and their ass on their shoulders before, began to smile at me—and taking them in the alley or to the park for some poon tang [sex] was as easy as plucking cherries from a tree.

'I remember the first time I had sex,' he told me, 'it was with this girl, ah, I think her name was Mary or something like that. I was about twelve or thirteen and I guess she was about the same age. I didn't really know what to do, but I'd heard some of the older boys talk about it and I remembered what they said. I guessed it must have been her first time too because I couldn't hardly get it in—but when I did it was *sooooo* nice, and man, when I got my nut I didn't know what was happening to me. It felt like a big explosion inside me, and the chick screamed at the same time.'

Jimi went on: 'I was very adventurous and promiscuous; and I really liked flashy clothes—even as a child. But my father being a gardener and not able to afford to give me the money to buy them, the only way to get them was to go into clothing stores after hours through the back window.'

He switched to another recollection:

'I was thrown out of school by a very sexy teacher when I was fifteen, for holding this white chick's hand. I know what she was *thinking*, but what she said was, "The classroom is not to be used for making amorous overtures to the girls in your class." So I said, "What's the matter? Are you jealous?" Out I went!

'After that I started working, helping out my dad because sometimes things got kind of rough, 'cause in the winter there wasn't very much grass to cut. Sometimes the cupboard was kind of bare, although I knew my dad was doing the best he could.

'I was good enough then on the guitar to start working with little groups that we got together. We really thought we were something, but we didn't do much more than play at parks and recreation centres for teenage dances. I remember the first gig that we did that we got paid for was at a place like an armoury or something. I think I ended up with about fifty cents.'

I asked Jimi what kind of music he was playing at that time.

'We played rhythm and blues,' he said, 'and things that were popular on the radio then. But I didn't get many chances to solo because all the guys were on ego-trips, so I just kind of stayed in the background.'

In another of these conversations we had where Jimi was looking back over his childhood and beyond, he told me about his biggest brush with authority from those years.

'It was the most frightening thing that happened during my childhood,' Jimi said. 'This friend of mine was a guy with a lot of nerve—one of these guys that was always trying to show off, you know what I mean? So one day he came by my house with this fine 'chine [car] and asked me if I wanted to go for a ride. I said sure and hopped in. He told me it was his uncle's car and I believed him. I should have known better because his family didn't have a pot to piss in or a window to throw it out of. Anyway, we were speeding along, laughing and talking, radio blasting, talking about what chicks we were going to pick up and take to the park to screw, when suddenly there were the fuzz. And there was I in jail for seven days until the guy that stole the car finally told them that I had nothing to do with stealing the car and in fact that I didn't even know the car was stolen. Man, my dad was angry at first. But he was cool when he realised I wasn't a car thief after all.'

At that time in America, of course, every male had to register with his local draft board on reaching his eighteenth birthday, and so be classified in one of the numerous categories. That was the ominous cloud of future uncertainty that hung over every young American guy's head. And there was a lot of wheeling and dealing going on in the local draft boards, to keep the sons of privileged, well-to-do, influential people from going into the government's two-year military service. It was typically American how, somehow, the majority of youths called up seemed to be from the black population and the lower-income-bracket whites. Now of course if you were going onto higher education, or you were attending a college or university, you qualified for a deferment. Which meant that you could enter military service later—if indeed you were called up at all—as potential material for the higher echelons of the military.

Since Jimi Hendrix had no such educational aspirations, he realised that he would be ripe for call-up at eighteen. And that probably he would end up in what was considered the most thankless branch of the military services, the Army.

The guys in the US Army were jokingly called Ground Pounders, due to the obvious fact that they mostly had to walk everywhere they went; and Jimi didn't consider that there was much glamour attached to being a Ground Pounder.

So when he was seventeen, he figured he would beat them to the punch. With his father's permission—which was necessary for enlistment at seventeen—Jimi enlisted in the US Airborne Paratroopers. The date was 1961, and he was accepted and sworn in as a paratrooper trainee in the 101st Airborne.

By mistake, he left his guitar at home.

'I felt,' he told me, 'as though I had left a part of myself behind when I forgot my axe'—a name he sometimes called his guitar—'so I wrote home and asked my dad to send it, and when he did I felt whole again. My guitar is a very important part of me.'

Jimi didn't meet Billy Cox until later when he was stationed at Fort Campbell Kentucky. He did, however, while undergoing his training, play in the military service clubs and in the cities surrounding Fort Bragg and Raleigh, North Carolina.

Jimi also did some playing in the town surrounding the camp and became very popular throughout that area.

Raleigh was like every other city that seemed to spring up near the military camps all over America—cities where the economy is dependent on ripping off the young, lonely kids sent out there for their military training—kids, for the most part, away from home for the first time.

Jimi remembered Raleigh like this:

'There were the sex-for-sale chicks waiting, and for five bucks you could get a quickie in some dingy room where if you didn't keep one hand on your pants while you were making it with the chick, you'd get ripped off for the rest of your bread by a mysterious hand through a hole that had been cut conveniently through the wall. And I can remember those sleezy bars with their neon signs blinking a welcome to all of us lonely suckers, and the urine-perfumed benches where you could sit with a whore straight from satan, buy her a drink and she would jack you off with one hand and lift your wallet with the other.'

It was a ritual that after you completed your training, you packed your own parachutes. 'They let you do that,' said Jimi, 'so that if they didn't open when you jumped from the airplane, you had no-one to blame but yourself!' We laughed about that and he went on:

'I had a little less than a year of screaming *aghhhhhhhh!* and *I'm faallliiiiing* all the time, so I squeezed my way out by breaking my ankle and hurting my back. Jumping from a parachute is the most alone feeling in the world. Every time you jump you're scared that maybe this time it won't open. Then you feel that tug on your collar and there's the big beautiful white mushroom above you and the air is going *ssssh* past your ears. That's when you begin talking to yourself again.' Jimi made twenty-five jumps altogether.

'After I split from that scene,' he continued, 'I tried being serious with my first love, music.' He talked about this turning point with that certain whimsical, humorous expression on his face that he got when he was reliving past incidents vividly.

'I joined a band after I blew all the bread I had when I was discharged from the Army Airborne. I blew it on—yeah, you guessed it—"wine, women and song", as they say in the best tradition of letting it all hang out!'

The next development Jimi recalled is one I remember as typically Jimi:

'We were working on a tour of the southern states, doing one-nighters, and I met this foxy chick, sexy to the bone—I spent a sleepless night with her. And, ummmm, I can tell you by that experience, the weather is not the only thing that's hot down there in the summertime. I just couldn't get enough—we were like two love-starved wild animals. It was really something. When we did finally fall asleep, long after the sun came up, I was so washed out that I overslept and the band bus left without me. I woke up and the chick had gone —back to her husband probably, to take her beating for staying out all night, and by now she was probably making love to him.'

The name of the group that left Jimi Hendrix behind— strictly in the geographical sense—was The Flames. He managed without them.

'There I was, stranded in some nameless southern town with no money, just my guitar. So I hitched a ride to the next large city and managed to get a job in a little jive-ass club.'

It was there that things started happening a little more, although for Hendrix it was mostly just frustrating.

A little more time passed and then a tour came through town with a bill that ran: B. B. King, Sam Cooke, Chuck Jackson, Solomon Burke, Jackie Wilson and Hank Ballard. Jimi was back in a job.

'I learned an awful lot,' he said, 'guitar-picking behind all of those names every night. Then in Atlanta, Georgia, I auditioned for Little Richard, copped the gig and worked with him all over the US.'

The trouble with that, though, was that Jimi and another member of the group tired of wearing the same stale uniforms and decided that they'd rebel and buy fancy shirts. Little Richard was not the man to do that to. That night, when he pranced on stage for his royal reception, dressed in the 3rd dimension of his brilliantly-coloured sartorial splendour, he gazed upon the two impetuous upstarts who had had the audacity to break precedent. That was the night he called Jimi Hendrix and his friend every name but the child of God over the PA system. That was the night Jimi Hendrix got the message that there was only one pretty boy on

Little Richard's show and that was Little Richard.

Oddly enough, Hendrix stayed on for a little while after that but split over a different disagreement.

'I quit,' he explained, 'because of a money misunderstanding. I finally landed in Los Angeles, California, and played with Ike and Tina Turner, and had a rest.'

But the frustration and impatience Hendrix was feeling all through this period ran far deeper than money or wearing uniforms or not being upfront on stage. It was the level of the music that was wrong.

'I had all the ideas and sounds in my brain,' he said to me, 'and playing all those other people's music all the time was hurting me. I'd jumped from the frying-pan into the fire.'

Jimi jumped again, this time to New York, where further frustration was waiting, though at least some work was waiting too.

'One night one of the Isley Brothers heard me playing and said he had a job open. Sleeping between them tall tenements was hell—rats running across your chest, cockroaches stealing your last candy bar, so I figured yeah, I'll gig.' (There is actually an album available with Jimi playing with the Isley Brothers: see the Discography at the end of the book.)

Years later, when Jimi's career was over, I visited the Isley Brothers and asked them what their opinion of Jimi had been during the time he backed them up. Ronnie Isley said:

'I especially remember that Jimi required almost no rehearsal to learn our songs. Jimi seemed also particularly gifted in duplicating exactly on stage the sound that had been on the recordings. And you know, even though he played exactly what we wanted to hear, he somehow seemed to be above and beyond that kind of music: because he played it so effortlessly.'

Rudolph Isley (the jolly one) said: 'One time when we took Jimi to our home in Teaneck, New Jersey'—which is in a very exclusive district, not usually accessible to black people—'I remember him saying that someday he would be able to afford houses like that. And everybody just laughed. Nobody really believed that Jimi's boasts would more than come true.'

But the brothers all said that they had been impressed with Jimi, that indeed he'd left a profound impression on them, and that above all he'd really struck them as an individual. Yes indeed . . .

Jimi's individuality, in fact, soon meant that, once again, he was unhappy within the confines of the Isley Brothers Band.

'I got tired of playing in the key of F,' he told me later, 'so I turned in my white mohair suit and the patent leather shoes.'

Another musician who remembers playing with Jimi at this time (he would play with him, later, on the recording sessions Jimi and I did in 1967) is Ray Lucas. Ray was drummer with the late great King Curtis, was a personal friend of mine and came to know Jimi personally too.

He remembers his first contact with Jimi like this:

'I remember I was playing at Smalls Paradise in Harlem with King Curtis one time, and our regular guitarist was sick, or in jail, or something, and even though I'd heard of Jimi, I'd never seen him or heard him play, so I was in for a hell of a shock. We didn't even have time to rehearse before the gig that night, and on a lot of songs that Jimi didn't know, the bass-player had to whisper the chords to him. But I never in all my fucking life saw anybody pick up songs as fast as Jimi did that night. It was a real pleasure to play with him—and, I'll be honest—I knew immediately that he was probably the best young black guitarist I'd ever seen. But I had no idea that he would become the world-famous superstar that he did. And the reason, partly, was that it was mighty damn hard for a black brother to be recognised, no matter how good he was.'

Jimi was indeed finding it hard—not only to be recognised, but even to get by.

Jimi remained in New York, back among the tenements and cockroaches, until he decided, no matter what the cost, that he would move into a cheap hotel. For a man with myriad musical ideas seething through his brain, the cost was indeed high—for it meant pawning his guitar, and later, selling it.

It was at that point in time that Jimi and I first met.

CHAPTER TWO

My life/intersection

I was born in Fort Scott, Kansas, on an Indian Reservation, of black and Blackfoot Indian parentage. My grandparents are still living on a Reservation near Beggs, Oklahoma.

My early childhood revolved around religion and the church, as did Jimi's. I started singing in various church groups when I was very young, and found I had inherited a talent for writing from my mother.

My mother's whole life was wrapped up in the church, and in love for others. She would wake up at all hours of the night, to write down poems and lyrics for songs.

She was also a keen observer of people's behaviour. I remember her taking me with her in our beat-up old car, down to the town square, where we would just sit and talk for hours, and comment on the people going past. We would just sit there in the car, sizing people up.

I really enjoyed that, and I think it started me on the road to people-awareness. At any rate, I found out later in life that I could get a pretty good first impression of the people I came across, good, bad and indifferent.

After Kansas, we lived in Colorado and Arizona. The news of my mother's death reached me in Phoenix, Arizona, as

I was cooking my breakfast before rushing off to school. She died during a routine appendectomy operation: someone had forgotten to bring the oxygen tanks into the operating theatre and, at the inevitable moment, they realised too late that my mother had stopped breathing.

That was the year I graduated from high school. I had about twenty offers of university athletics scholarships, but for some reason the result of having a big row with my aunt was that I decided 'to hell with going to university'.

That left me with national military service looming up, and I was even less keen on doing that. I wanted no part of the US Army—forever training and crawling on your stomach and sleeping in mud. Not for me.

The only way out was to join another service voluntarily, so I enlisted in the US Air Force, which took me to North Africa, Europe and Japan. Japan was a source of endless fascination to me—so much so that I taught myself Japanese so that I could get into the heart of the country and really communicate with its people.

I was in California when my honourable discharge came through—so I figured I'd stay there a while and see what I could get going.

I sang with a group there long enough to make one low-budget movie called, if I remember it correctly, *Pop Girl*. It wasn't exactly nominated for any Academy Awards, but it was a lot of fun doing it. And working with the group almost kept a roof over my head and food on the table: black-eyed peas, 16 cents a pound. A big potful lasted a week or more. I used to see them in my sleep.

It wasn't too glamorous a life, at that time. The Los Angeles police were getting very heavy. A walk down the street after ten o'clock at night was a guarantee of being hassled. You didn't have to be doing anything, you just had to be there and be black. They'd be cruising along on the west side and they'd spot a couple of black brothers and zoom—

they'd drive right up onto the sidewalk to get you. They were mostly recruited from the southern states, and they weren't overly fond of, or gentle with, black people. They reminded me of Hitler's SS troops.

It got me down—it seemed like the writing was on the wall, that my future was not in California right then. I caught a Greyhound bus, with precious little in my pockets beyond the fare, and rode it all the way to New York City. You have to be irresistibly drawn somewhere to travel 3,000 miles on a bus to make it; and drawn I was, in a way and with a force that I have never understood.

This was early 1963, when I arrived there, checking into the YMCA with my beat-up guitar and little else besides hope. I didn't realise how tough it was going to be. The rent at the YMCA was cheap, and it saved me from sleeping in Central Park—but I became a resident of the park after a while, when my money ran out altogether.

I started making the rounds of clubs and musicians' hangouts, trying to get a band together. One by one I got musicians that I thought would sound good together, as a unit. I found a booking agent, got him interested in the group, and convinced him that given a chance we could do a good job.

I was experimenting with different kinds of sounds and rhythms—fusing Indian music with blues, religious music with rock—trying to find something new. People liked it, and the group built up a circuit in the city and the surrounding areas, and we got to working pretty steadily.

About then, a friend told me that Ed Chalpin was looking for singers. I went down to his studio for an audition, not knowing what to expect; but he heard me sing, and heard some of the songs I'd written, and asked me if I'd be interested in a recording situation with him as my manager. I signed.

Shortly after that he bought his own modern 10-track

recording studio at 1650 Broadway, on the corner of 51st Street, and called it Studio 76. The building was known as 'the music building' then, because it had lots of record companies and music publishing firms all crowded together inside it.

And then suddenly, as if all the things I had done and the steps I had taken had had, unknown to me, a specific and pre-destined purpose, came the next event ...

CHAPTER THREE

The Big Apple

It was 1964, and Jimi also felt drawn towards New York City—the Big Apple. (Rotten to the core, but irresistible.) He also arrived with very little money—and found that, in order to check into a cheap hotel, he had to pawn his only possession, and his first love, his guitar.

The hotel, which has now been torn down and replaced with a parking-lot, was on West 47th Street by Times Square. And this was the place that destiny had chosen for our meeting.

In the lobby of the hotel there was a small recording studio, and I stopped by there one day on an impulse. Standing by the elevator, and giving off the most beautiful vibrations I had ever felt, was Jimi Hendrix.

I had the strong feeling that I had been in this place and this situation before. It was truly as if all the past events of my life had been leading up to this moment. I walked over to him and said hello, and I asked him what he did.

'I play guitar,' he said, 'but I don't have my guitar. Things haven't been too good. I had to pawn it and then I had to sell it, to eat and pay the rent—and even now, my rent is overdue again.'

For those of you who may not be familiar with the un-scrupulous practices of hotels in New York City, let me enlighten you as to the system. They have what they call a plug, that they put in your door when you're behind in your rent. It is actually half a key, and once it's inserted in the key-hole, there is no way to unlock the door except with the other half of the key: and guess who has that other half of the key. Anyway, possession being nine tenths of the law, it was a cat-and mouse detective game when you were behind with your rent. By law they couldn't put the plug in your door until they caught you out of it—so the bell-hop was forever sneaking and peeping, the enemy hiding around the corridors and corners, listening at doors, waiting for the moment that you would leave, so that he could swoop down like a vulture and put that plug in your door. If that hap-pened, you were forced, if you had any belongings, to go to the desk and get issued with the supreme ultimatum: pay up or lose your belongings.

Such was the situation looming over Jimi's head when we met.

He told me that he didn't know why, but he'd felt a com-pulsion to sneak down to the lobby, even at the risk of being plugged out by the bellhop.

I said that I happened to have two guitars—I'd just bought a second from a friend who needed the price of a ticket to California: he was quitting the Big Apple, taking the oppo-site trip to mine. I told Jimi that if he would go back and wait in his room, which was on the seventh floor (which meant that the two of us added up to the number nine, which is a very significant number in the life and death of Jimi) then I would bring up a guitar and amplifier and listen to him play.

I felt even then that there was something special and momentous about this occasion. I rushed out to my car and got the guitars and amp, walking through the lobby under the glaring scrutiny of the desk clerk, who would certainly have thought I'd just stolen the guitars had he not seen me going in instead of out.

Totally unprepared for what I was about to hear, I knocked on Jimi's door and went in. There, lounging on his double bed I could see this very beautiful chick of about nineteen. This was my introduction to Fayne Pridgon, Jimi's main chick at that time.

Jimi plugged in the guitar and amp, and it seemed almost like one single movement, and as though he were someone just reunited with a long-lost love. He was, of course, a left-handed player, so he had to turn my guitar upside down in order to play.

In a matter of minutes he did things with that guitar that I had never imagined possible.

After I managed to come down and catch my breath from the brief but timeless trip that he took me on, what seemed like a journey to all the celestial heights of this universe, I told him that the guitar he was playing was my gift to him, and that if he wanted he could be my lead guitarist from that moment on. He looked at me with a depth of understanding I had never encountered before—and this was the beginning of the many happy hours, weeks and months I was to spend with Jimi Hendrix, a person from another time and another place, sent to us as a messenger of love, peace and freedom.

We found that right off we had a beautiful musical rapport, and that my writing—Jimi himself wasn't into writing at that time—gave him inspiration and a basis for figuring out great sounds and arrangements. Songs came to me as they had done to my mother. She left me with a gift for lyrics and melody that will always keep her spirit with me. About two days after I met Jimi I went running to his room in excitement, and with a feeling of release, because I had managed to take care of his rent situation. The threat of the plug in the door no longer existed.

I burst into Jimi's room shaking with excitement. I felt that I had written the one song that expressed the deepest feelings of my oppressed people—the first black rock protest song, in fact. The song was called *How would you feel?*, and the lyrics ran like this:

If you walked into a restaurant and you had the money to get yourself something to eat,
and somebody told you to go round to the back door to get it, even though they weren't gonna give it to you free
—tell me how, how would you feel, if you were me?
You take your little children by the hand;
all you want to do is guide them and protect them on their very first day of school:
I just wanna ask one question
—do you think that all the little children should be punished, for the sins of all the other fools?
How would you feel if you were me?
You walk to the corner, you stand at a place called the bus stop;
the bus pulls up and the man opens the door, yea;
he might look at you funny but he takes the money,
and then he says hey, you're not one of us
—sit in the back of the bus.
Tell me how, how would you feel, if you were me?
One more thing I wanna tell you!
You pick up the morning paper and you read about people fighting and dying in some foreign land:
but right here people are fighting and dying—
and all they're trying to do is get equal rights as the Constitution planned.
Tell me how, how would you feel, if you were me?

That was the first new song I wrote after meeting Jimi. 'Hey,

Jimi, listen to this!' I said. And immediately, he picked up his guitar and started playing it, playing along as if he knew the song before I even sang it. (One of many mysterious things that happened during our association.)

We were both very thrilled at the outcome of our combined efforts, and both felt that the song should be recorded immediately.

So I took Jimi to see Ed Chalpin, recognising the fact that Jimi and I together had something new to say, and hoping that the public would accept it on records. Ed Chalpin signed Jimi to a recording agreement—the first one that Jimi had ever signed—and we went into the studio to record.

It was the first time Jimi had ever recorded in a studio where he had complete artistic and arranging freedom, and his instinct and his versatility amazed me. At this first session Jimi played every instrument except the drums. He arranged all the instrumentations and even sang vocal background with me and another friend. We thought the session turned out fantastically well, especially since we had got down *How would you feel?*.

We were able to get this track released as a single, and the record company had great hopes for it, because it was one of the first of the rock protest songs. The music trade papers commented that it was important, timely, and a record that should be heard. However, in its efforts to get the record played on the air, the company found itself in all sorts of difficulties because the radio-station managers considered it 'too controversial'. So to this day, *How would you feel?* has never really been heard in the United States.

In the meantime, in other fields, our success was growing. As we continued to experiment with different sounds our reputation as a good rock band was expanding along the East Coast.

I remember one place in New Jersey where we used to play a lot. It was called 'George's Club-20', and it was so crowded that we could hardly get off the bandstand—that is, on our 20-minute break out of every hour. But we dug it all the same, even though it was always filled with smoke and the smell of chicken and barbecued spare ribs cooking in the kitchen. That chicken was greasy, but it tasted good after a few hours of playing over a pallid, inadequate PA system.

Jimi usually had his pick of the most attractive girls that crowded round the bandstand to watch him do his tricks with the guitar. He was up to all those tricks back then —playing with his teeth and his tongue, and manoeuvring the guitar into all kinds of sensuous positions that made the girls practically come out of their dresses.

Many was the night that he would say to me at the end of a gig, 'Well, ah, Curtis, I don't think I'll be riding back to the city with you. Someone has invited me for breakfast.'

It was at about this time, too, that Jimi first met the late great Devon. Tall, voluptuous, beautiful, Devon was the first supergroupie that Jimi was to come into contact with. She too had been born in Seattle, Washington, but she and Jimi didn't meet until they had both moved to New York City.

Few groupies are sufficiently confident to climb to the very competitive plateau of being a supergroupie, but Devon was a person determined to make it; and she did.

There were a number of things about Devon which Jimi felt attracted to : she was, above all, magnetic; and she was also attractive, and totally into sex—proficient, imaginative —from A to Z. And around her there was always a bevy of other foxy ladies. But Devon was also good for Jimi's head, for she was one of the hippest black chicks Jimi was to meet, with far above average intelligence and a knowledge of the drug scene that was incredible.

'I introduced Jimi to his first acid trip,' Devon said, 'and he liked it a lot. He tried various pills with me and our relationship became one of excitement and exhilaration. He sniffed cocaine, but he had no desire at all to get into heroin at that time, because he knew that this was a one-way street that led to nowhere.' Ironically enough, Devon was later to die of a heroin overdose—and more ironic still, to do so at a time when she was filming a movie in New York about heroin addiction.

'I was attracted to Jimi's flamboyance,' Devon said of their early relationship, 'even though at that time he wasn't an established star. He had a certain visible flair about him, his hair was longer than any other black musician's that I'd ever seen, and in an original style; and he had Star Potential written all over his musical abilities.'

We began to get into better clubs, and then played a certain club in Manhattan almost all the time. The place was so packed that if we didn't get in there early, there was no way to get in at all, because the people who came clung really tight and stayed a long time. We both believed in putting everything into our performances, and we felt that pleasing the people was food for our souls.

That was always an impressive thing about Jimi : he was never on an ego trip. He always had time to rap with anyone who wanted to ask him something about music or whatever.

At this time Jimi really loved Greenwich Village, and we used to spend a lot of our time there, just walking around and digging all the groovy heads.

Equally, some of the grooviest of people were digging Jimi too. Miles Davis, the jazz star, remembers seeing Jimi at that time.

'The first time that I saw Jimi play,' Miles told me, when I talked with him six years later, shortly after Jimi's death, 'was in 1965, at a club called The Lighthouse.' (The Lighthouse was one of our 'home-bases'—our regular clubs.) 'That club was about two minutes' walk from my house, and I used to stop in there for a drink. Even then I could see genius and scope in Jimi's playing—he went in all directions making his musical statement. And I was amused by Jimi's stage antics, because at that time, even in rock groups, the visuality trip hadn't really happened. Plus, of course, in strict contrast to what Jimi was into, the jazz scene had always been identified with coolness. Me too.

'But in many ways Jimi and I were alike—because my unpredictability has gotten me many unwanted headlines, yet actually only increased my popularity. Because it's been proven over and over again that the public loves a controversial figure, especially when there's undeniable talent to go with it. So I had a kind of unseen bond with Jimi—because even back then, Jimi was controversial: and he certainly had undeniable talent.'

That talent was growing every day.

We landed a regular gig at the 'Cheetah' club, which at that time was on Broadway and 53rd, and was considered *the* club in New York City. It also paid the most money, so all the groups were trying to work there.

The only way you could do it was to audition. The Cheetah was owned by some French people who now own one of the grooviest discothèques in New York. They were pretty hip, but I don't think they were quite ready for what Jimi did when, after six other bands had played, it was finally time for our audition.

We had Jimi on lead guitar, I was playing rhythm and singing; we had an organist, bass and drums—and it was very together. We played the first song and they really dug it, and about halfway through the second number Jimi started playing with his teeth, tongue, behind his back, between his legs. I was dancing as if my legs could fly. They stopped us right there in the middle of the song and said 'You got the job!'

The club itself was huge, with an upstairs and downstairs, separate Music and Grooving rooms, and the most elegant bathrooms you have ever seen. The couches and wall décor were in a fabric that really looked like the coat of a cheetah.

And there were lights and reflectors everywhere, making the whole place look like something from outer space. It was the gathering place for people of all ages, people who were into dancing and wearing way-out clothes. It was always packed out.

Jimi and I thought we'd better get some of those way-out clothes ourselves; we went down to the Village and found some material that was almost the same as the décor at the club, and we designed ourselves shirts and jackets out of it. We added white bell-bottoms, and we looked like we were coming out of the walls.

By this time, Jimi and I writing and playing together had created a new sound, different from anything our audience had ever heard. I was sharing some of the lead vocals with Jimi, but mostly I did the singing, because Jimi really preferred just to play his guitar. That is the way Jimi wanted it. He liked to concentrate on his playing, and he didn't think he had much of a voice.

It was about this time that Jimi began to experiment with certain drugs: pot, coke, an occasional up, but nothing too heavy. He was basically a highly curious person, always wanting to find out for himself where something was really at. However, at that time, he quickly left alone those things he found he couldn't handle. He found that he dug smoking pot and sniffing coke more than anything else, and therefore that was what he stuck to.

It was also becoming apparent, more and more, that Jimi was deep into numerology, and he possessed a vast knowledge about other planets that someone would have to live about nine lifetimes to acquire. And indeed Jimi was fascinated by reincarnation, and told me many times that he had been here before in other forms and as other people.

One night I woke up from a dream so real it was as though it was a vision of future destiny. I realised that I had been given a look into Jimi's future. In the dream I saw but one colour—mauve—the colour symbolising the blending of all colours, beautiful and tranquil. Through a mist of mauve I saw Jimi, very content, but in a spirit form unlike anything I had ever seen or imagined. The vision signified to me that Jimi was really where he belonged, and on his face was registered a complete and total happiness.

When I woke up from this dream, I went straight to Jimi and told him about the vision, and what I had seen in it. He looked at me very strangely, not speaking for a long time. Then he said to me: 'Curtis, I want to tell you something. It is now 1965, and I will be dead in five years' time: but while I am here I will travel many highways, and I will, of necessity, die at a time when my message of love, peace and freedom can be shared with people all over the world.'

I had never been so moved as by this dream and Jimi's grave, soft-spoken words, and at once a song began forming in my head with such force that it appeared to have been there all the time, just waiting to come out.

This was September, 1965—almost five years to the day before Jimi's death—and the song I wrote was called *The Ballad of Jimi*. The lyrics run like this:

Me and my best friend
Travelled down life's highway
We talked of how,
How things should be,
Of peace and love for you and me.

Of a life without hate,
Of a life filled with love.

On that first day he played my guitar
Somehow I knew he'd travel far
Reach out and find his distant star

Many things he would try
For he knew soon he'd die.

Oh why did it happen,
Oh the sadness we must face
Why did it happen
If I could but erase
All the tears that were shed,
All the heartache and the pain.

That is my story
It has no end.
Tho' Jimi's gone
He's not alone
His memory still lingers on
Five years, this he said.
He's not gone
He's just dead.

When I finished the song, Jimi liked it so much that he
insisted that we record it right away. And he insisted on
playing all the instruments at this session, and he overdubbed
the different instruments many times until he got the sounds
he wanted. In the end, he had played everything on the
recording except the drums, and had even sung with me on
the harmony.

The record has never been released in the United States to
this day. It has, however, been released in Europe—in Britain,
Germany, Holland and Italy—and in Australia. Shortly after
Jimi's death, I was invited to Paris by the Pathé Marconi
Record Company to sing *The Ballad of Jimi* on national
television as a tribute to my friend Jimi Hendrix.

In Britain, the song was issued as a single after Jimi died,
and many pop writers and fans assumed that I was ripping
off Jimi's memory with a commercial death-song written

after the event. Nothing could have been less true, as Jimi's own voice on the recording testifies.

Jimi spoke to me many times about things I really didn't understand at the time: about his being sent here from another world as a messenger, and about how we must suffer and reach a certain spiritual height before we would be allowed a permanent place in the spiritual world. I did, however, realise that some of life's mysterious forces were guiding our destiny, because so many things had happened that made me aware that Jimi Hendrix was no ordinary person.

Our band continued to work the most popular clubs in and around New York City, and sometimes we found ourselves auditioning again.

One of the most popular clubs in the city in late 1965 and 1966 was a place called 'Ondines', which was located on East 59th Street, directly below the 59th Street Bridge.

It was the favourite hang-out of British groups who were beginning to come over to the USA in ever-increasing numbers, and one of the groups that went there a lot was The Animals—who were one of Britain's biggest acts and pretty popular in America too.

I had become very used to people admiring and rapping with Jimi about his playing, because he was indeed something to hear and see, but The Animals paid him unusual attention. While we were playing Ondines, they would come back night after night and spend most of their time talking to Jimi in a corner.

I began to feel that something strange was going on, because every time I went near the table where they were talking with Jimi, they would either stop talking altogether or change the conversation abruptly. This went on all the time we were working at Ondines.

When we finished there, we had about three days off before we were scheduled to go back to play at the Cheetah.

Suddenly, Jimi disappeared. He had checked out of his hotel; none of his many girl-friends had seen him. It was as if he had vanished into thin air.

The next time I heard of Jimi was a few months later, when I read in one of the trade papers about the new, wild sensual guitar phenomenon of Europe, the leader of 'The Jimi Hendrix Experience'.

Jimi had been talked into going to Europe and promised fame, money and more besides. He was still supposedly my lead guitarist, and he was still under legal contract to Ed Chalpin. But he had gone; and he had left without a word to me or to anyone I knew.

CHAPTER FOUR

London Bridge

'In New York when I joined up with Joey Dee and The Starliters, ... mind you, this is an outasight group, but!!—after sucking on a peppermint twist salary, I had to quit. Began playing with a juke-box band, and quit that too, with nothing but a Wish Sandwich— two bits of bread wishing I had some meat to put between them. Came to England. Picked up two of the best musicians: Noel Redding, formerly of a group called the Loving Kind, for bass; and Mitch Mitchell, an ex-Blue Flame, on drums. Formed the Jimi Hendrix Experience. Now I'm gonna make certain I don't fluff it up.'—JIMI HENDRIX.

As you know, that is indeed what happened—but there is a great deal more to the story than that.

Jimi arrived in England in the latter part of 1966, little knowing that he would set the rock world on fire, first in Britain, then Europe, then America and the rest of the planet —and that he would more than do justice to the name 'The

Wild Man of Pop', which was to be bestowed upon him by writers and fans alike: indeed by everyone who encountered this 21st Century phenomenon.

Jimi himself, though he may have had his visions, did not envisage such a future for himself. In fact he was deeply apprehensive about the reception he would get. He wasn't by any means sure that his style of playing, and his musical ideas, would find an acceptance in Britain.

It was an understandable apprehension, in the context of what was happening in America at the time, both musically and socially. The music scene in the States in '66 was chaotic, and the pressures of racial prejudice were very strong—and were polarised particularly at the time as the result of the long overdue federal enforcement of schools integration.

Those were the situations that Jimi was familiar with, and he was uncertain as to whether he would find them duplicated and harder to deal with on unfamiliar shores.

Chas Chandler, however, had no such doubts. Chandler began his career up in Newcastle, where he became the bassist in the original Animals. When he saw Jimi Hendrix in Ondines in New York City, he felt that here was someone for whom it would be worth changing over to the role of manager. (He is now the manager of Slade; he certainly can spot potential.) Chandler believed right from the start that Hendrix could make it if he started off in Britain, and that given the right promotion and publicity, and given also carefully hand-picked musicians behind him, there would be virtually no limit to Hendrix's success.

So here was Chas Chandler cast in the unfamiliar role of manager, with not much in the way of financial resources, but with a world of talent in Jimi Hendrix and with a faith in him that matched that talent—a faith that was to be the main thing that kept him going through the difficult early stages of getting Jimi off the ground.

From New York, Chandler very wisely alerted the attention of all his acquaintances in the music business to the fact that he was going to bring Hendrix over to London—which very successfully created an air of expectancy and interest in advance.

When Jimi arrived at the airport, he was driven, right after the customs check-in, to the private home of Zoot Money, one of Chandler's friends, for an immediate extended jam session. Years later, Jimi recalled this with pleasure, telling me how much he had appreciated Chandler's thoughtfulness—for the jam had let Jimi into things gradually and informally, and yet since it had happened so promptly after his arrival, he was at once given a boost to his confidence with the opportunity to introduce himself by means of his forte, his guitar. 'It was a really nice welcome to England,' said Jimi.

After the jam, Chandler and Jimi checked into the Hyde Park Towers Hotel, where the real business of getting things together began.

The first priority was to get a couple of dynamite musicians to accompany Jimi. Noel Redding explained how he joined the Experience :

'I was either nineteen or twenty. I had my guitar and had gone to London to see about a job. I probably had about ten bob' (a dollar twenty) 'in my pocket at the time, and I saw an ad in the *Melody Maker* that the Animals were looking for a guitarist. So I figured I'd have a go.

'The audition was at a place called the "Phone Booth", but anyway after I got there and played, I found they'd already selected a new guitarist for the Animals. But Jimi was there, and he asked me if I could play bass, and showed me the chord structure to a song I'd never heard before. The song was called *Hey Joe*.

'I remember I was very hungry, and I remember Jimi

buying me a drink and giving me some candy. I'm not sure,
but I think he also gave me about ten bob. After we played
the song for a while I was feeling happy, because he seemed
to like the way I played and he told me to come back the
next day. And that's how I got the job. And I figured that
if I was going to play in his group it was just as well that
I play bass, because I couldn't see anyone else playing guitar
with this black bloke.'

Jimi was being very selective, and especially so about
potential drummers. He told me: 'None of the drummers
that I listened to made me feel like playing, and that was part
of what I was looking for. Someone to make me feel like
playing. I had to feel the right vibrations.'

Mitch Mitchell was reportedly one of the best up-and-
coming young drummers in Britain at the time, but had just
left Georgie Fame's band, The Blue Flames. A nice irony
followed, in that Georgie Fame was to become one of the
earliest and keenest admirers of the Jimi Hendrix Experience.

At any rate, Mitchell had a lot of potential, and was to
prove exactly what Hendrix was looking for. He had a
colourful free-form style of playing that complemented perfectly the style and structure that Jimi envisaged. Mitchell
also had the advantage of having and playing a double kit—
which was welcomed as an added source of visual appeal and
musical power for the band.

I talked to Mitch about how his attachment to the
Experience came about when we rapped backstage together
at the Pocono Pop Festival in Philadelphia (which was held
on a site weirdly close to Muhammad Ali's private training
camp); Mitch said he remembered little about it. 'All I can
recall really is that I heard about these auditions being held
for this unknown black American guitarist, and I decided to
go along.' But Jimi himself remembered a great deal more,
and described it to me in detail.

He still had traces of a shocked, amazed expression on his face when he was relating to me his thoughts and feelings the first time he saw Mitch Mitchell:

'Man, when I saw that small young dude sitting behind that big double drum-kit of his!—I didn't think he could reach the cymbals. But when he started to play I knew I'd found the drummer I was looking for. Because not only did he play with power, which I was looking for, but he had a very original style which I knew would go very good with my own kind of playing.

'He played a lot of fills and different types of rhythms, that I felt would be very necessary in a three-piece group. I didn't want a fourth instrument,' said Jimi, 'because it would get in the way of the arrangements of the music I had in mind. I needed a disciplined type of bassist who would not overplay but be content to play certain bass lines that I myself would work out—because it would be the job of the bass to hold the group together, while the drummer and I would be playing a free-form kind of style within structured arrangements. So we would need the bass playing a kind of simple rhythm, so that we would be able to go and come back musically and the basic rhythm would still be there.'

I asked Jimi if part of the reason for selecting Noel Redding had been his red hair, because I knew that Jimi was really into colours, and into having a very visual act. He said no, there were just two reasons why Noel had been chosen.

'First,' said Jimi, 'he played what I considered a steady bass, and second I felt that I could communicate with Noel, and that was a very important consideration in putting my group together.'

So that's how the Jimi Hendrix Experience got picked— and that first, tentative time that the three of them played together was an auspicious and promising occasion: they played four solid hours without stopping. It felt right, and it obviously *was* right.

Mitch Mitchell
    Born—John Mitchell, Ealing, London, 9 June 1947.
    Appearance—5′ 8″ tall; brown hair; light brown eyes.
    Family—parents Phyllis and Jack Mitchell; no brothers or
        sisters.
    Education—Ealing College; Corona Academy.
    TV Début—*Jennings at School*, 1960.
    Other Work Done—Ovaltine advertisement, 1967;
    Instruments played—drums; congas; percussion.
    Previous groups—The Riot Squad; Georgie Fame's Blue
        Flames.

Noel Redding:
    Born—Noel David Redding, 25 December 1945.
    Appearance—5′ 9″ tall; red hair; brown eyes.
    Family—parents Anthony and Vicki Redding; no brothers
        or sisters.
    Education—Folkestone Grammar School; Folkestone Col-
        lege of Art.
    TV Début—*Ready Steady Go*, December 1966.
    Instruments Played—bass; guitar; violin; banjo.
    Previous groups—The Loving Kind.

When I talked, years later, to Eric Burdon, he remembered that first get-together of the Experience like this:
    'I was rehearsing musicians to put a new group together, and Jimi was just sitting around—just checking things out. A guitar-player came in for a job, and he played for me and I said "Don't call me, I'll call you". As he was leaving, Hendrix got hold of him and said "D'you play bass? Will you play bass?"—and of course that was Noel Redding.
    'Then the two of them played together—and that was the

first time I ever heard Jimi play. (They just jammed in the cellar.)'

I asked Eric what his first impression of Jimi had been at that time, and he told me:

'The first impression was that he was too hot to get close to. I mean too complex and too simple to get near to. In a forceful way I just realised I would have to check him out and look at him and kind of watch him work—and that eventually a relationship would come out of it. Because, you know, I could see immediately that everybody was buzzing around him because he had so much force. And then with Chas being my ex-bass player and being Jimi's manager, there were a lot of times when we would cross each others' paths, at parties and things like that.

'In fact Chas offered me part management of Jimi. He wanted us to be partners managing Jimi. But I was, well, I was doing my own music. I was making my own album at the time, and I could tell that Jimi was a devil, you know. So really, to take care of somebody like him, you know— you really got to be able to sit on him for twenty-four hours a day, man. You got to take care of the guy. And that wasn't my trip.

'So I just coasted behind, watching him work and eventually we got to have record evenings together, when we would just play records all night long after the Speakeasy closed and everyone else had gone.'

I asked Eric whether, from that first early contact, he thought that Jimi would get to be as big a star as he did indeed become.

'Oh, yeah,' said Eric. 'I checked out with the chicks that had seen him first. I didn't listen to the music particularly at first. I listened to my old lady and I listened to the chicks around saying that he was the heaviest force around for a long time. Well, not in those words but the way chicks say things—like "Wow, this guy—this guy's outta sight". Or like my old lady put it. She said "Out of all the music that's come out of the rock era, Hendrix's music conjures up what I would like to hear a group sound like more than anything else." She said that to me and I thought yeah, right. He *is* that heavy, you know?'

Eric went on:

'So, like I said, I really backed off at the beginning—not giving him any kind of deep attention because it was just too heavy. And then later when Chas Chandler brought round the tapes of the first album and played them to me—when we finished listening to it, man, I just—well, it wiped me out.'

Chas Chandler, of course, was 'wiped out' earlier than that—right from the first rehearsal of the group, he knew he had a winner of real size.

After just three days' rehearsal, and with an understandably limited repertoire, the Experience had to play their first gig: from nowhere right to the Paris Olympia. Jimi had sat in with Brian Auger at a club in London called 'Blaises' one night and was heard by France's own Cliff Richard, Johnny Halliday. Like everyone else who stumbled across Hendrix in England at that time, Halliday was impressed and got them a gig at the Olympia very promptly indeed.

'We had to carry our own equipment,' Jimi explained. 'There was no way we could afford roadies then. No-one had ever heard of us and we didn't know many songs. So I would play real long solos and then eventually come back to whatever the original riff was in the song. I was really surprised that we went over so well, because we certainly didn't have much rehearsal.'

After the Paris début, the Experience returned to London for more rehearsing, and to get a more extensive repertoire together. At the same time the search was on for more gigs and for a suitable record with which to launch the group.

But things were getting tight at this point, despite all

Chas Chandler's faith in what he had. As Hendrix later recalled:

'Gigs were scarcer than hen's teeth, and I knew that Chas was fast running out of money. He had already sold some of his guitars to keep us going.'

It became necessary for Chandler to find some more finance and some better business connections, and to do this, he had to sacrifice a proportion of his 'shares' in Hendrix. He did a deal with Mike Jeffries whereby Jeffries brought in a lot of money and a lot of business contacts and acquired 50 per cent of Chandler's management deal with Hendrix.

That settled, the need for a recording deal and a record release was urgent. But it was left to Chandler to hustle it all through, and according to what Jimi himself told me, Mike Jeffries was never around, never available, at this time. Perhaps this was the first—it was certainly an almost immediate—point of dispute between Jeffries and Chandler. At any rate, such disputes grew until eventually Chandler felt forced out, sold his 50 per cent to Jeffries and dissociated himself altogether.

Back in these early days of the Experience, however, it was Chandler and Hendrix who were working together— Chandler and Hendrix who established a rapport with each other which at times was strong enough for Hendrix at least to attach a spiritual significance to it.

One such instance was in the way that *Hey Joe* came to be selected as the first Jimi Hendrix Experience record. Chandler had picked up a copy of the song recorded by Tim Hardin—it was originally recorded by a vocal group called The Leaves—when he was over in the USA previously, and had brought it home with the vague intention of re-recording it. Unknown to him, Jimi had already alighted on the song, worked out his own very different arrangement and decided he was keen to cut it.

'There's this song I thought of doing called *Hey Joe*,' they said to each other. So it became the agreed and obvious choice.

Chandler decided to rent a studio, bring Jimi down with Mitch and Noel, and produce a recording himself. He was sure it would turn out impressive and exciting—and he was sure he'd be able to sell it to a major record company.

He was right about the first part, and wrong about the second. The recording of *Hey Joe* went fine, presented no problems, and exceeded both Chandler's and Jimi's expectations. But their mutual feeling that they had a great cut and a potential commercial hit were not shared by the first major company to which Chas Chandler offered the tape.

Decca Records, who had turned down The Beatles, turned down Hendrix also.

'They said,' Jimi told me with the amused superiority of hindsight, 'that they didn't think it was commercial enough. *They* didn't think *I* was commercial enough!'

All the best people get refused first. George Martin saw the potential in The Beatles after Decca had shown them the door; John Hammond recognised that certain something in a twenty-year-old kid called Bob Dylan after a Vanguard Records executive had declined to offer him a contract; and likewise when Decca turned down Jimi Hendrix, Kit Lambert picked him up.

It was then that Jimi first met Pete Townshend of The Who. Remembering that first meeting, Townshend told me:

'Our manager, Kit Lambert, said, one day, that he was gonna bring this guy down to the studio, and said to me that I was sure to like him, and surely get on well because there were lots of sort of parallels in the way we played. Well anyway, we were recording at IBC, and we were doing some dumb number at the time, and Jimi sort of wandered in looking peculiar, just really peculiar, and Keith Moon was in a nasty mood and said, "Who let that savage in here?" I mean he really did look pretty wild, and very scruffy. Anyway, he walked around for a bit, and gave me a sort of luke-warm handshake, and then I never saw him again for a little while. I didn't know anything about his playing, and I never heard his music until I saw him first live.'

Scruffy or not, Kit Lambert saw to it that Hendrix was taken on by Polydor Records and then by his own subsidiary label, Track Records.

By coincidence, it was also Polydor that was in the middle of negotiations at that time with Ed Chalpin—my manager and still holder of a legal recording agreement with Jimi— about releasing the first song recorded by Jimi and I (cut October 1965): *How would you feel?*

(People have often asked me how *did* I feel—how did I feel when Jimi Hendrix, whom I had helped financially and as a friend, who was contractually my lead guitar-player and signed—as a result of my efforts on his behalf—to a record deal in New York City—how did I feel when he just disappeared to England without a word, breaking all those American contracts and promises?

The answer is truthfully that I never looked at it that way. I never thought that I had 'discovered' Jimi Hendrix, and I knew that he'd get success without my help. I never meant for the little ways I assisted him to put him under any restraints or obligations; and I knew that though he had been my friend, he was also destined to be everybody's idol, and a law unto himself.

In any case, Jimi and I were later reunited, and reunited at Jimi's own behest. When he returned to the States, after conquering Britain and ascending to the pinnacles of stardom, he called me up and asked that we record together again. And thus it was that Jimi and I went into the studios again, recorded again, laughed and talked and shared some good times again. And thus it was too that Jimi told me those parts of his story that I hadn't lived through with him, in many, many conversations which I can still hear, vividly, in my head—and which it is the purpose of this book to pass on to you.)

So. Understandably, Polydor came out with *Hey Joe* and quietly forgot about *How would you feel?*, even though every instrument on that recording is played by Hendrix except the drums, and the drummer is Bernard 'Pretty' Purdie, who is now renowned the world over as a session-musician extraordinaire, and is Aretha Franklin's musical director.

After the recording deal was finalised, Chas Chandler saw to it that the pieces began to fall into place, with Jimi and the Experience getting the maximum exposure possible in the shortest amount of time. Knowing the British scene as he did, Chandler was sure that Hendrix would have a tremendous impact on the current crop of established stars, and that with their acceptance, and their inevitable influence on others, he would be a star without much further loss of time.

And that was what happened. As Pete Townshend told me, 'Jimi fairly blitzed London,' and the frequent club appearances in London's trendiest places quickly paid dividends with unprecedented press coverage, as from December 1966.

'Now hear this,' wrote one reviewer, who caught Hendrix's act at the Bag O' Nails club, a gig which Chandler spent nearly the last of his money on. 'And hear it good. Are you one of the fans who think there's nothing much happening on the pop scene? Right—then we want to bring your attention to a new artist, a new star in the making, who we predict to whirl around the business like a tornado.'

The piece was headed 'Mr Phenomenon' and continued singing Jimi's praises at some length :

'His name is Jimi Hendrix; occupation—guitarist, singer, composer, showman, dervish, Original ...

'Jimi was in full flight, whirling like a demon, swirling his guitar every which way. This twenty-year-old looking like James Brown (Soul Brother No. 1) was quite amazing. Visually, he really grabs the eyeballs with his technique of playing the guitar with his teeth, his elbow, rubbing it across the stage—but he also pleasurably hammers the eardrums with his expert playing. He has an astonishing technique.'

And certainly the other musicians on the scene thought so too. Pete Townshend and Eric Clapton, two of the country's most brilliant guitarists, went to hear Hendrix every night they could. They followed him round, so impressed and captivated were they by the achievements and expertise of this palpable rival for their crowns. Pete Townshend told me:

'I saw him first at the "Blaises Club", and I was going in as Jeff Beck was coming out, and Jeff Beck said to me, "He's banging his guitar against the amp. You'll just have to tell him that's your thing." So I went in and listened, and of course he was doing a lot of the things I used to do, like banging his guitar around, and he was using lots of high feedback. But he was also playing in a way that I couldn't hope to approach. You know, for me it was a bit like a dream come true to hear that guitarist. It was very peculiar Eric and me always going together, because Eric was one side of the coin and I was the other, and we used to go and watch Jimi who was like an embodiment of the two styles that we had.

'And then he took it from there on. I don't think I've ever had as much enjoyment out of a live performer as I have out of watching Jimi, because I felt so free just looking at him. I've always had this thing about Charlie Parker, and I've really liked his music. I felt that listening to him you felt sort of liberated within, that he was free and flying. And you got that with Jimi. If you gazed at him while he was playing, you could sort of go with him and feel very free.

'But Jimi played in every club in London—every single club in the space of ten days. Eric Clapton and I saw every show, every single one, except for two we missed because we literally couldn't get in the door. Towards the end he was getting really famous....

'It was a big, big, big surprise of course. You know, everybody gets used to the idea that there are incredibly talented black bands in the States, backing up people like Little Richard, and lots of backroom boys, as it were, that the public never get to see. So you expect the occasional miracle, but you also think that they're gonna stay in the background a lot. Now, when Jimi arrived, he'd gone through that kind of schooling and that kind of suppression, and whether it was that it sprung directly from a sort of prejudice situation—or not a prejudice situation but a situation that was too tight for him, I don't know, but when he did get over here, he definitely did explode all at once. It was like you were getting all that ambition and all that, you know, energy, all happening. And it all happened in fucking ten days—you know, I was telling you that he played roughly three clubs a day.

'I think his being black helped that "jump off". All that pent up energy exploded. Everybody was dumbfounded, I mean, some people reacted. My reactions would differ. Sometimes I'd just give up and say, "Yea, he's the greatest thing that's ever happened", and other times I'd feel a bit mean that he was using the kind of stage gimmicks that I was using. But later, of course, I think that he was one of the most universally accepted musicians, by musicians, that I know of, because he used everything that there was to use.'

The rock press, too, was impressed right across the board. There was a unanimity of praise from all the music papers. They raved, they picked up on both his virtuoso abilities and the visuality of his act, and they provided the public with a well-defined image of this exciting new performer:

'The man for whom the words "Wild One" were invented has hit us,' wrote one columnist. 'Hendrix is a one-man guitar explosion with a stage act which leaves those who think pop has gone pretty with their mouths hanging open. What this man does to a guitar could get him arrested for assault.'

It seems that everyone had discovered what good copy Jimi was. Hence, for instance, a review of an early Hendrix appearance at Bromley, Kent, which carried the title 'Sex and Gimmicks and Jimi' and included these observations:

'Two electric guitars continued happily emitting sounds as Jimi Hendrix left the stage at the Bromley Court Hotel last week. Considering the number of indignities the instruments had suffered during the preceding forty-five minutes, I wouldn't have been surprised if the instruments had gotten up and made a speech.

'Jimi's reputation had preceded him into Kent, and a large part of his audience had gone along to see exactly what tricks he did get up to. One observer said,

'"More and more often during his act, I was reminded of the early days of The Who, when Pete Townshend was at his most violent—except that Jimi takes it several stages further ..."'

And Jimi's own comments to the press at this early time only served to keep the publicity ball rolling. He was suitably vague, suitably self-confident, and suitably determined to have a ball.

'I've only been in London three months,' Hendrix told reporters, 'but Britain is really groovy.' And: 'We don't want to be classed in any category. If it must be a tag, I'd like it to be called "Free Feeling"—it's a mixture of Rock Freak Out, Blues and Rave music.'

Did it hurt to play guitar with his teeth? 'No,' said Jimi, 'but I do have to brush my teeth three times a day.'

Did he rely on the sex angle for his on-stage impact? 'No,' said Jimi again, 'not really. I guess there is some sex, but I don't plan anything. I just do what I feel at the time.

Gimmicks? Sure. We don't work things out though: we just let them happen.'

He also started a little reminiscing with the British press-men:

'I remember when I got my first guitar,' he told them. 'After one month I wanted to join a band.' And again: 'I remember when I got out of the paratroopers and played down south, on the west coast, and then in Washington, we had guys ten years ago in the States playing what groups are playing here now, only now they call it psychedelic!'

Meanwhile Chas Chandler was also talking to the music press, though somewhat more modestly—indeed, with a strange lack of exaggerated hype, considering his position as Hendrix's manager.

'We're waiting for a full work-permit,' Chandler explained, 'but now we hope to get Jimi work in the big clubs, building up a following. You can watch him seven nights on the trot and he changes individual items each time. You can't get bored with him ... Believe us, Jimi is really something positively new; we think he'll become a sensational success ... he has this unique stage appeal and this mastery of the instrument.'

Chandler, of course, was right. And in a sense, Hendrix was wrong: wrong, that is, to imply that the British scene was ten years behind the American. If anything, the situation was the opposite: Chandler had brought Hendrix to Britain recognising that Jimi's advanced playing and technique would be more readily acknowledged and appreciated in Britain than in Jimi's home country.

And certainly that recognition came—and came, as Chandler had gambled on it doing, initially from the other stars of the day. The jobs, actually, were slower coming than Chandler and Hendrix had hoped, though the Experience did land a £25-a-night gig as support band for the New Animals around the clubs in these early days. What mattered most, at this juncture, was the attention of the stars (and so too of the music press)—and, of course, the progress of the record *Hey Joe*.

It was released by Polydor Records in December 1966, and on 14 January 1967, it came into the British singles charts at Number 24, despite, in fact, very little airplay until that point. Jimi was still being paraded on the London club scene, and the gigs at the Bag O' Nails were beginning to really pay off, as this press report from January '67 demonstrates:

'Jimi set the swinging London club scene alight last week with a stage act that left big pop names on their feet shouting for more. In the audience at the Bag O' Nails, rapidly becoming the new "in" club in town, was a galaxy of stars, including Beatles Paul and Ringo, with Brian Epstein, Rolling Stone Bill Wyman, Hollies Allan Clarke and Bobby Elliot, Pete Townshend of The Who, and John Entwistle, Eric Clapton of Cream, Lulu, the Small Faces, Donovan, Eric Burdon's Animals, Georgie Fame, Geno Washington, Tony Hall and ex-Moody Blues singer Denny Laine ...

'Jimi looks set to become one of the brightest stars of 1967.'

Indeed.

January saw *Hey Joe* climbing up the charts, and more press coverage, and more attention by 'the right people', came with it.

'Off-stage,' one paper reported on 28 January, 'he's nervous, shy, gentle; but performing, Jimi Hendrix is the wildest thing on the London club scene. The most obvious thing about Hendrix is that he is not pretty—and neither is his raw brand of beat music. But this has not stopped him from setting the pop music world by its ears. The perceptive Mr Jagger has dropped into a late-night club to hear his brilliant guitar antics, and Mr McCartney has invited Jimi back to a little evening soirée, with John Mayall and Marianne Faithfull. In short, the Jimi Hendrix Experience is happening on the London club scene.'

And as *Hey Joe* climbed the charts, the general public too began to feel that Hendrix was 'happening', and while it was becoming more and more obvious that Jimi had 'arrived', nobody really had any idea just where he had arrived *from*. But the press, as usual, was ready to give people answers, and Jimi himself was not averse to providing little potted biographies whose interest was not reduced by mere in-accuracy.

This was a sample from *Disc* 1967:

Jimi's Favourite Things:

Home: 'I now share a flat with Chas Chandler. It used to belong to Ringo. In fact they only took the drums away the other day. There's stereo all over the place, and a very kinky bathroom and lots of mirrors.'

Favourite Food: 'Spaghetti, strawberry shortcake with whipped cream, and banana cream pie. I like typical soul food too—greens and rice.'

Favourite Drink: 'I still like milk, once in a while. Scotch and coke, rum and coke, and American root beer.'

Pets: 'I love animals. Deer and horses are the prettiest. I used to have dogs and cats as a kid—I used to bring a stray dog home every night till my pa let me keep one. Then it was the ugliest of them all! It was really Prince Hendrix but we just called it dawg!'

Cars: 'With all these backward streets I don't think I could drive here. I had one back home but a girl-friend wrecked it, she ran it straight through a hamburger joint. After that I started to devote more time to my music than to girls.'

Ambition: 'To be known as having a particular sound. I'd like to be recognised for my music the same way as some-one like Chuck Berry.'

Records: 'Some Motown records are good, but I really dig the blues—though only when I'm alone and can really listen.

I like Elmore James, Robert Johnson—he's so cool—and the very early Muddy Waters. That sort of music gets the message over, and comes through so easily.'

Fears: 'Sitting right here, you can't last forever, I hope I won't lose my gigs. I'd like to go from one gig straight onto another. If I write something about three or four in the morning, I can't wait to hear it played. It's even a drag to have to wait for the other cats to arrive. It's like being almost addicted to music. Music makes me high on stage, and that's the truth.'

Marriage: 'I almost did that the time of that car incident. With music there's no time for anything else, I'm already married to my music. You'd have to work a whole lot of voodoo on me to get me married. A girl tried once, crazy cat. She put a lock of her hair in the heel of my shoe. I had to go see a doctor afterwards. You wouldn't think these sort of things happen, but I can tell you it's real scary when it does.'

Hobbies: 'I used to like to paint at school. The teacher used to say paint three scenes, and I'd do abstract stuff like Martian Sunset, no bull!!'

Politics: 'All I know is what I read in the papers. I don't care so long as they don't drop the bomb before I get a chance to make money!'

Smokes: 'If I didn't smoke I'd be fat as a pig. My nerves are very bad. I like tipped cigarettes mostly, alternating with menthol ones—about a pack over a day and a half.'

Religion: 'There are so many different beliefs that something must be phoney. I used to go to Sunday School, but the only thing I believe in now is music.'

Dress: 'Most of the time I get hung up on one particular thing, and can't stay out of it. I don't want to ever look at a tie again. I had enough of shiny suits and patent leather shoes when I was with an R & B band. Clothes like that restrict your personality, you're just one of the other cats.'

Likes: 'Thunderstorms. I like to watch the lightning,

especially on the fields; and flowers when I'm on my own. Science-fiction : it's about the only thing I read. I read anything I can on Bob Dylan though.'

Dislikes: 'Flashy people and flashy conversation.'

Favourite Colours: 'Black, and blue.'

It was said by many of the top pop commentators of the day that at the time of Hendrix's emergence, there was little direction in Britain, nor in Europe, nor indeed in the USA. What was needed was an injection of something radically different, to provide a new impetus, to find the parallel lines from confusion to infinity. Jimi Hendrix was the captain of that spaceship.

He was the most visual, sensual and dynamite artist to hit pop music since Elvis The Pelvis Presley, and he had extra dimensions, including sheer volume. The Experience soon had a reputation for its earth-scattering volume, though this actually served the specific purpose of allowing Jimi's space music its special impact and its special effects. So too, Hendrix quickly established himself as the king of feedback (although, of course, unknown to Hendrix, Pete Townshend had been very much into guitar feedback before ever Jimi came to England).

With all these ingredients for appeal and success, and with the record of *Hey Joe* a hit, it was now possible for the group to be booked in concert halls throughout the country. They started out playing second or third bill and really began in a significant degree to build up their cult-like following.

The début of the Jimi Hendrix Experience outside of the club scene was in February (1967) at the Savile Theatre on a Sunday night, on a bill topped by The Who. Hendrix was in great form, and emerged from the evening as an acknowledged star.

'Jimi brings the roof down', one write-up was headed, and went on to provide this eulogy :

'The Who, it was rumoured, had threatened to raze

London's Savile Theatre to the ground in their bill-topping act last Sunday. Fortunately, they didn't—it would have been a terrible waste of an excellent showplace—but instead the roof was nearly brought down by the power-packed excitement of Jimi Hendrix ...

'Jimi is surely the musical phenomenon of recent times. His popularity—on the strength of just a few appearances, the odd TV spot, an unusual record and lots of talk—has rocketed with a force seldom equalled in the world of pop.

'Here's a musician to the very core, a guitar genius who plays with incredible feeling and fervour. If he never gets another hit disc, his showmanship and those wild electronic exercises on stage will carry him through.

'Despite early amp and mike mishaps, it was his night, from *Rock me Baby* through a knockout *Like a Rolling Stone* and *Hey Joe* to his version of *Wild Thing* ...

'Even the incredible Who, themselves veritable leaders on the sound scene, seemed hard put to follow this tousle-haired giant.'

Indeed, I got confirmation of this impression from Pete Townshend himself. He told me:

'It was OK at the Savile, it was good. But I felt a bit edgy about it. I said to Kit Lambert, our manager, "It's just that we shouldn't be playing with somebody of that class. They shouldn't be our backing-group. It's not that I can't stand the competition—it's just that I can't stand the competition!"'

At this point in time, according to what Jimi told me later, all the decisions involved in the management of the Experience were being taken still by Chas Chandler alone, and Mike Jeffries was never around.

Chandler was steering Hendrix carefully, and after the resounding success of the Savile Theatre appearance, he decided that the Experience could benefit from more exposure to different audiences before they went on their first proper British tour. The solution was a five-day tour of Belgium, which was also highly successful.

Chandler had the choice of four different tours of Britain. One of those he declined to put Hendrix into was a projected tour with—again—The Who. He chose instead to take up an offer from Dick Katz, then of Harold Davison's agency, for Jimi to tour with the current sex-idols of Britain, the Walker Brothers. Also on the bill were Cat Stevens and Englebert Humperdinck.

Chandler felt that this would be the most advantageous tour, because it was heavily rumoured that the Walker Brothers were about to split, every date on the tour was sold-out, and Jimi would have more chance of stealing the limelight than from the more talented and dramatic Who.

This first and vital tour for Jimi and his band was, ironically, the last tour of its kind, with a star-studded bill catering to many divergent tastes in pop; and it is not hard to understand why Chandler chose to do it.

'I can just hardly wait to do it,' said Jimi, relishing the prospect of fitting into a tour with the Walker Brothers like a hippie at a vicarage tea-party.

Yet actually this mischievous spirit alternated, for Jimi, with moods of doubt and apprehension.

'I'm a bit worried,' Jimi admitted, 'about the type of people who's gonna see the tour. If they come to see the Walker Brothers then they're not gonna want us. I just hope they listen.'

If they didn't, Hendrix figured he'd just go ahead in any case, because even if it didn't please others, his music certainly pleased *him*.

'If they do scream for the Walker Brothers during our act,' he said, 'I'll just ignore them and play for myself.'

It was not, in any case, the first time Jimi had been involved with package tours. He had played behind a string of big-name artists all over the USA, as we've seen from an earlier chapter. And sometimes there too, tour managers and promoters lumped together on one bill incongruously disparate acts.

'Like The Beach Boys and James Brown on the same tour!' Jimi remembered.

Chandler, in any case, knew that all this admixture of artists on the Walkers' tour would only serve to increase Hendrix's impact. You're going to upstage the other acts, create controversy and grab headlines, he told the Experience beforehand—and he was right.

The twenty-five-day tour kicked off on 31 March at the Finsbury Park Astoria, and as soon as Hendrix and his band got on stage, they were beset by amplification and mike problems, and would have bombed right there and then in front of the overflowing audience, had they not been such a visually arresting and musically immaculate act. In the face of these problems, Hendrix did indeed 'play for himself', blasting through his act regardless.

Well—not quite regardless, because in fact although Jimi disliked having to go through pre-planned routines, and preferred to behave on-stage entirely as the mood took him, he had, on this occasion, been impressed very strongly by his management with the need to create a new sensation—to surpass anything that had been done on stage before.

They hatched the famous diabolical guitar-burning scheme, designed to present something truly dynamic and dramatic for the little girls waiting to scream at the Walker Brothers.

'They just suggested it would be a good scene for the group,' Jimi told me later, when we talked about the tour in some detail. 'You know—it would help our popularity, if I did something really spectacular on stage. And most of the obvious things had been done. Like some guy was supposed to have pulled his pants down on stage, and then he was supposed to have turned around and showed his smiling cheeks to the crowd. Well, I am not into that. Also I heard some guy pulled it out and flogged and whacked it, right on stage in front of a packed audience. I wasn't about to do something like that either.'

Jimi went on: 'Anyway, I didn't really like the idea of doing *anything* that was already planned, even if I did have the perfect song for that scene—which was *Fire*—because whatever I do, I like for it to just happen.'

Nevertheless, when it came to it, Jimi felt like destroying his guitar anyway—or so he said.

'That night we were really receiving a luke-warm reception, and I'll admit something needed to happen. Me and this guitar had been in spiritual conflict all evening anyway. I told it to do one thing and it did another and I was really fed up with it. I wanted to kill it. So when they poured the lighter fluid over it I was glad because by then I was ready to tear it apart with my bare hands.

'At first I couldn't get the matches to light, but finally it went up with a big burst of flames like a mini meteorite striking earth. The crowd really freaked—they loved it. But the theatre manager and the other officials flipped out. I thought for a while they were going to arrest me or at least put me in Happy Acres [an asylum]—I almost burned myself up, and one of the roadies, in that fiasco. I also think I succeeded in awakening some inner range of cosmic consciousness within that fucking guitar.'

The incident was picked up by virtually all the pop music publications, and in many cases succeeded in getting the Experience their first front-page colour coverage, and helping substantially the burgeoning of Jimi's popularity.

It was not the only controversial incident on the tour. Many of the theatre managers were uneasy enough about Hendrix's onstage behaviour, without the extra provocation of burning guitars.

Some early pictures of Jimi: *A*. Jimi as a baby; *B*. age 2; *C*. with brother Leon; *D*. age 3; *E*. age 5; *F*. in football uniform with uncle; *G*. with father, playing mock football, 1956; *H*. a drawing by Jimi of a Rock Superstar; *I*. with classmates – age 10; (*continued overleaf*)

(*from previous page*) *J.* asleep in his father's house, 1968; *K.* age 18, US Army Paratroops; *L.* a group he played with in the South (USA), after Army Medical discharge; *M.* arriving at Seattle airport, 1968; *N.* with his father, brother Leon and step-sister, 1968; *O.* with father in Seattle

Me with the Squires. Jimi is on the left

Top: Background vocals, first recording session of *How Would You Feel*, 1965. 1650 Broadway, New York City. *Bottom:* George's, Hackensack, New Jersey, 1964

Club Cheetah, 53 Broadway, Times Square, New York City, 1965

Top: Queen's Inn, Queens Boulevard, New York City, *1965. Bottom:*
Ondines, 59th Street and 3rd Avenue, New York City, *1965*

Listening to playback, Jimi Hendrix at his first-ever recording session.
Curtis Knight sitting, Johnny Starr, extreme left, Jimi Hendrix –
cigarette in hand – Ed Chalpin, engineer George

At the Purple Onion, 4th Street, Greenwich Village, New York City, 1964

Top and bottom: Me performing. *Middle:* Concert for Attica – Yoko, John Lennon, Curtis Knight – at Apollo Theatre, 18 December, 1971

On 8 April, Maurice King, the tour promoter, announced to the press that Rank Theatres had complained to him about the act, saying that if Hendrix didn't 'clean up' his act he would be banned from their theatres on the tour. King also said that he had in fact spoken to Hendrix, who had agreed to change his act.

Whether or not that was the case, it obviously wouldn't have looked very good for this new, cool, black anti-hero to be meekly acquiescing to clean-up-your-act demands from local businessmen. So Chas Chandler quickly denied the Maurice King story, and Hendrix's own comment was a classic pop-idol quote that re-echoed all Elvis Presley's comments of a decade earlier when *he* had been in trouble over *his* stage act. What Hendrix said was: 'I'm just bemused by the whole thing. All I want to do is sing and play my guitar.'

When pressed, on another occasion, to explain why playing his guitar included playing it with his teeth, his comment was rather more extravagant: 'I got the idea,' he said, 'when I was down in Tennessee. Down there you had to play with your teeth or else you got shot. I left trails of broken teeth all over the stages.'

In any event, by the time the tour was halfway through its run, Hendrix was a star, and important pop news. In mid-April, a French TV film unit arrived at the Ipswich Odeon theatre to film the Experience in action—which not only added to the general impression that Hendrix was indeed upstaging the stars of the tour, the Walker Brothers, but also reflected the dramatic impact which Jimi's music was having on the French rock scene. Hendrix in fact opened up the whole psychedelic music era in France, and provided a focus for those French kids who were already, by that time, into hallucinogenic drugs and who needed a spacey, fluorescent music to go with it.

Giles Pétard of the *Record World* in France wrote afterwards that 'Jimi Hendrix brought an era of music and love to France that will never die'.

The tour itself was gruelling, but the sequence from the Ipswich date shown to television viewers in France, showed, as did every other night's performance, no loss of energy on Jimi's part.

'This is like a rest for me,' he explained, 'after the hectic life of constant club work. And,' he added, 'I really hate to lose out. You can't blame me for being selfish by trying to get our songs across to the public as quick as possible.'

Yet it was by no means all success and invaluable publicity. Specifically, he had to have four stitches in his foot after a fuzz-box foot control broke during his show at Chesterfield on 15 April, though he managed to go on for the second house later that evening. (That was another way in which those tours were arduous: there were always two shows a night.)

And more generally, Jimi was unhappy at what he considered was a systematic sabotaging of the Experience's performances—little, vicious acts of revenge for the show-stealing achievements of the group. As Jimi explained it afterwards to me, he felt as if there were a group of destructive ghosts travelling with them every step of the way— ghosts who were so good at making their presence felt that by every honorable rule in the book they should have been co-featured artists.

'I know that I'd just finished tuning my guitar and then by the time I'd walk in the dressing-room and come back, a string would be broken, or the guitar would be mysteriously out of tune,' he told me, adding that 'there were other times when these damn gremlins would get hungry I guess, and eat one of the tubes from an amplifier, or we would be playing and suddenly all the power would go out.'

Hendrix tried hard not to let it get him down, and indeed came to gather a kind of strength from it—until, indeed, it actually started working *for* him.

'One time the scheme really backfired on their smart asses,' he recollected. 'I was really into a solo and I was humping my guitar and the audience was really getting off on it and suddenly the amplifier blew up!—but instead of it stopping the show, spoiling everything, as it was meant to do, it only served as a fantastic climactic ending to what I was already doing. And I told those mother-fuckers that the only way they were gonna get rid of us was to throw us off the tour.'

That didn't happen.

The tour proceeded and finished on schedule, and Hendrix came away from it in a much stronger position. In the first place, he had measured up British audiences accurately enough by the time it was over.

'I really learned a lot about British audiences on that tour,' he said, 'because every night we had two more to meet, and after each show Chas and I would discuss how everything went down, and ways to improve. It was a gas, in spite of the hassles.'

In the second place, the tour had earned him a considerable amount of publicity, as we have seen; and in the third place, Jimi's recording career had skyrocketed in the interim.

The single of *Hey Joe* had reached the number 4 position on the British charts, and *Purple Haze* had been issued as a follow-up—this time on Kit Lambert's own Track Records label. The B-side was, like *Purple Haze*, a Hendrix composition—*51st Anniversary*—and it is indicative of Jimi's increasing confidence in his own musical and popular future that he was already dropping from his repertoire most of the songs written by other people, retaining in his act only his immensely popular and successful versions of Bob Dylan's brilliant *Like a Rolling Stone* and Reg Presley's old Troggs' hit, *Wild Thing*.

The reviews for *Purple Haze* were good, if a little tentative. One reviewer, and his comment was typical, wrote that the record was 'not to me as instantly commercial as *Hey Joe*, but ... rather a stronger showcase for this wild-haired talent, that groaning guitar and that fury-tipped voice'.

The record arrived in the charts on 4 March—that is, before the start of the tour with the Walker Brothers—at the number 39 position. From there it went up, not with any astonishing speed, but gathering a notable momentum: 32, 22, 11, 6, and then, a fortnight later, on 6 May, to its highest position, number 3. At the same time it had featured heavily in the more specialist R & B charts, where it rose to a top position of number 4 on 13 May.

At the risk of over-saturation, a third single was issued and joined *Purple Haze* in the charts, so that the music papers for 20 May showed *Purple Haze* still riding high at number 10 and the new single at number 15. The same day, Track Records also issued the first Jimi Hendrix Experience album, *Are you Experienced?*

The single was called *The Wind cries Mary* (backed by *Hi Way Chile*) and showed a heretofore unknown dimension in Hendrix's work. It was a very beautiful expressive ballad played and sung by Jimi with a tenderness and sincerity that many people had not thought him capable of achieving.

The album was rush-released only two weeks after the issue of *The Wind cries Mary* because although a later release-date had been planned, a couple of thousand copies of the album had inadvertently been leaked out to shops in the Midlands, and Track Records were keen to circumvent the possibility of black-market trading and the bootlegging of the album at exorbitant prices. (There were, later on, of course, to be considerable problems, from the record company's point of view, when bootlegging came, in 1969-

71, to be in itself a mass-market industry. The so-called 'legitimate' companies claimed, indeed, that bootleg records were costing them £100 million per year—though how they worked that out is not altogether clear. In any case, there undoubtedly was a very large amount of bootlegging activity at the end of the 1960s, and Hendrix, since he enjoyed a 'cult' popularity—enhanced even more by his death—was prominent among those artists who provided the most saleable grist to the bootleggers' mill.)

The rush-released album of May 1967 contained, when it emerged, not quite the selection of recordings which had been suggested by Jimi's announcements to the press. The album contained *Foxy Lady*; *Manic Depression*; *Red House*; *Can you hear me?*; *Love and Confusion*; *I don't live Today*; *May this be Love*; *Fire*; *Third stone from the sun*; *Remember*; and *Are you Experienced?*.

Jeremy Walsh, reviewing the album in *Record Mirror*, was not alone in saying that while an album written and composed entirely by Hendrix himself was admirable, none-theless 'he should have featured a couple of more familiar songs, maybe *Wild Thing* and *Like a Rolling Stone*, for example'.

And actually those particular numbers—established favourites in his live repertoire—had been intended for the album just a few weeks prior to its finalisation. Hendrix, taking a comparative rest after the tour, had talked rather more fully than before to the music press, on the subject of his then forthcoming first album and much else besides.

'Up to now,' he told the papers, 'I've written about 100 songs—but most of them are in those New York hotel rooms I got thrown out of. When I go back I'm going to collect them from those hotels where I missed the rent.

'I'm not ashamed to say that I can't write no happy songs. *Foxy Lady* is about the only happy song I've written. I don't feel very happy when I start writing.'

Asked specifically about the album, he had this to say:

'This album will be different, and all the songs will be mine except for *Like a Rolling Stone* and maybe a Muddy Waters number. We like to have our own sound.

'I'm writing a number—*I don't live Today*—it's really weird, man; I hope we can get it ready for the LP.'

Hendrix also told the press at this time that one of the tracks that in fact emerged on the album—*Love and Confusion*—had been intended as the second single—the follow-up to *Hey Joe*—before he came up with *Purple Haze*; and he gave out, too, a tantalising little preview-description of the then forthcoming *third* single, *The Wind cries Mary*:

'We've had two little records and I'm just wondering how the people are going to take the next one. I think everyone will think we've used different instruments, but it's still two guitars and drums. At one point the guitar sounds like a flute. I recorded it exactly as we do it on stage—everything we do on record, we can do on stage. If we had a disc with a violin on it, we'd hire a violin-player to come on stage for that one number.'

That was by no means all Jimi Hendrix had to say to the press in the brief lull after the Walker Brothers tour; nor was there any let-up in how much the press had to say about him, from descriptions of his hair and his then-fashionable military attire to the printing of readers' letters of abuse (on the group in general) and scepticism (as to whether the teeth-playing was a fake).

'Did you see Jimi Hendrix on *Top of the Pops*?' demanded one irate pop fan. 'Didn't he look weird?—it just isn't true! Now long hair's OK, but his looks quite horrible, standing on end like that. It was back-combed to a ridiculous extent. And his drummer, Mitch—those terrible towelling-patterned trousers, that striped shirt and the jacket with a map of America on it, ugh! If that's supposed to look nice, I give up. I don't get it; if you're that talented surely you don't need gimmicks. Imagine walking down the street and bumping into those three ... It's not very hard to learn to play an instrument but it is hard to be a good entertainer.'

Another wrote that 'He's a fantastic showman, and I was knocked out when I saw him locally. I enjoyed his forward rolls on stage while still belting out his music, but I'd like to point out to his fans that I don't really think he plays his guitar with his teeth. I have a group and we're one of the hundreds with a guitarist who is on the Hendrix/Clapton kick and we think Hendrix just turns his amplifier up full blast and puts his guitar over his face and doesn't touch it with his teeth but just plays it by moving his fingers over the fretboard; and because he is very loud he gets a sound without using two hands. He's still great, though.'

Modest, too, according to at least one paper, which ran a piece headed 'Jimi doesn't think he's a big name' and went on to inform its readers that: 'His appearance is striking. Heads turn as he passes—tall, black military jacket with ornate braid, wild and shocking black hair, Dylan-like. A face hewn with character. Yet Jimi Hendrix, guitar virtuoso, is modest. He doesn't regard himself as a big-name artist yet.'

Elsewhere, readers were also informed that 'Songwriter Jimi Hendrix has a fertile imagination that doesn't discount the existence of UFOs or life beyond death—an imagination weaned on Science Fiction, poetry and painting'. Jimi was quoted as explaining:

'At school I used to write poetry a lot, then I was really happy. Like in school, my poems were mostly about flowers and nature, and people wearing robes. And then I used to paint a picture of, say, a really pretty mountain, then write about four lines of poetry about it. I don't hardly get a chance to paint now. The girl in the office bought me a paint-box, but I haven't had a chance to buy paper. I like to paint different things, but I don't like to paint people.'

Hendrix also talked to the music press about the immediate future, about TV miming, about making songs out of his dreams, about the British music scene, and—as Zappa would say—'green things in general'.

The immediate future:

'Britain is our station now. We'll stay here till the end of June, then we'll see if we can get something going in America, and then we'll come back here. We'll be staying here off and on all the time.'

On having to mime for certain television pop shows:

'The one thing I'd hate to do is mimic a record—it's so phoney. So far the only thing I was asked to mimic was a Radio London appearance, and I felt *guilty* just standing there holding the guitar. If you want to scream and holler at a record, then you can do that at home. I'm strictly a live performer; I know I can't sing'—this was a recurrent theme of Jimi's, and was questioned over the years not only by ardent fans but by many of the more serious reviewers also—'I'm primarily a guitarist. Some people think I'm good and that's what I want to find out.

'I've been working with myself and my ideas for twenty-one years: now I want to find out from everyone else if they *are* any good.'

(That last comment alone indicated how fresh a talent had arrived on the established music scene—in which it was far more generally fashionable to offer up the theory that no-one except the star himself was in a position to fully understand, and therefore judge, his work.)

On dream-based songs:

'I dream a lot and put a lot of my dreams down as songs. I wrote one called *First look around the corner* and another called *The Purple Haze*, which was all about a dream I had that I was walking under the sea.'

I couldn't help thinking back, when I came across this quoted remark of Jimi's, to that fateful day in the New

York hotel in 1965 when I had gone to Jimi with the account of the dream *I* had had in which he had appeared to me not quite in a purple haze but, as recounted earlier, in a mauve mist. It seemed an ironic confirmation of the belief both Jimi and I always held, that providence plays strange tricks.

To return to Jimi's comments to the press in April 1967, and in particular to his remarks on the British music scene as he found it:

'You have a lot of groovy groups here in England—but some of the sounds are just too clean. You can't expect deep feelings to come out of music put down on bits of paper with arrangements. I *feel* everything I play; it's got to be inside you.'

On his special interest in science fiction:

'I want to be the first man to write about the blues scene on Venus.'

On his hair:

'I wear my hair long because that's the way I like it. It was long in New York but it's longer now because young people here are more open-minded in their attitudes.'

On his fondness for military jackets:

'Some people have told me that they think wearing a military uniform is an insult to the British Army.' (!) 'Let me tell you I wear this old British coat out of respect: this was worn by one of those cats who used to look after the donkeys who pulled the cannons way back in 1900—this coat has a history; there's life to it. I don't like war but I respect a fighting man and his courage. Maybe the guy who wore this coat got killed in action. Would people rather the coat be hung up and get mouldy somewhere to be forgotten like him? Men like that should not be forgotten, and if I wear this coat, I remember. Anyway,'— with a sudden smile—'I wear it because it is comfortable.'

And finally, on smiling for the camera:

'Do you know my biggest problem? I just can't look straight in the camera and smile if I don't feel like smiling. I just can't do it, man, it's like being told to be happy to order.'

It can't have been a very large problem—the photographs of Hendrix not smiling were successful enough, and contributed all the better to his image of sullen sexuality.

And that was no problem at all. The first time I met Jimi, back in New York City, there had been a beautiful naked girl in his bed; now, in these first heady months of his conquest of Britain in 1967, his special attractiveness to women was one area in which the reality he was living corresponded perfectly with his image. To talk to, Jimi was a gentle person, quiet and reflective, despite his public persona of brashness, wildness and even violence; but there was no such gulf between his private life and public persona where his sexuality was concerned.

The press, of course, dealt only with Jimi's sexuality in terms of his image, his public life—noting (they could hardly have missed it)—his patent suggestiveness with the guitar, his flagrant use of his 'axe' as a vast phallic symbol literally throbbing with power, aggro and flash. Yet mention of his private self, in terms of sexuality, was, perhaps rightly, taboo. This was before *Rolling Stone* magazine pulled all the stops out with its notorious groupies issue—before, in fact, the days of the new rock realism in which it was to become almost obligatory, especially in the more hip magazines, to deal in great detail with musicians' sexual predilections, dope habits, and so on.

In those early days, then, it was legitimate to 'reveal' that behind the Hendrix image of wildness and pseudo-violence was a soft-spoken, personable guy, and many of the music papers waxed quite eloquent on the subject. A typical piece at the time informed its readers that meeting Jimi 'in his den, manager Chas Chandler's London flat, with the rest of the group sprawled about ... is a chaotic, disconcerting experience—for the ferocious Jimi Hendrix on stage, with his attacking guitar-work and singing, is very much quieter and more easy-going at home than you'd have any right to expect ... he pads around quietly, answering questions in a quiet voice, but firmly, with little hesitation, with an air of "I've been around, and I'll tell you what I think, but I'm not gonna shout about it".'

As for the private Hendrix sex-life which the press avoided discussing, there is actually little to record beyond the fact that in the first place, he was, as had been the case in the USA throughout the time I knew him, doing OK for himself thank you very much, and that in the second place, he had by this time met the very beautiful and 'special' Kathy Etchingham.

Kathy came from Derby, was an old friend of Chas Chandler's, and met Jimi at the fashionable Scotch discothèque in London. Later in this book, Kathy talks in detail about the depth, the controversy and the beauty of their relationship—a relationship that began with Jimi kissing Kathy unexpectedly and gently on the ear.

The important point, at any event, was that at this point in time, despite the sudden mushrooming of his success, and despite too his continued intake of the drugs he had long been into, Jimi's personal life was relatively uncomplicated and unproblematic.

At any rate, it was a lot simpler and easier for him to deal with than it was later to become.

Jimi felt contented—even managing to remain cool and detached about the undercurrent of racial prejudice which, despite its lack of dramatic proportions compared to what he, like other black brothers in the USA, had suffered, was nevertheless there as a daily impingement.

'Soon as I arrived over here,' Jimi explained, 'I shared a flat with Chas, and immediately complaints started pouring in. We used to get complaints about loud, late parties when we were out of town on a gig! Come back next morning and we'd hear all the complaints. Chas got real mad about it—me, no. I don't let it bug me very much.

'Sometimes,' he added, 'some kids will shout something at you while you're waiting for a taxi on the corner; otherwise it's OK—everything's fine, I guess. I don't worry much about the whole scene anymore. Man, I'd even play South Africa, as long as there wasn't any physical violence—and if they tried to get me in other ways, I just wouldn't take much of it. Anyway they can only call you names. I just don't give a damn as long as I have beautiful England to come back to.'

But it wasn't, happily, only England that wanted Hendrix. After a rest at the end of the Walker Brothers' tour, and while his singles and his album were dancing around up and down the charts (the album reached the Top Three in the LP charts and the R & B Album Charts, and was only held off the national number 1 slot by the unbudgeable *Sgt. Pepper* album by the Beatles) Jimi and the Experience took off on a hectic month of touring in Germany and Scandinavia.

The press had quoted Hendrix as saying, 'There's so much I want to do—I want to get colour into music. I'd like to play a note and have it come out a colour—in fact I've got an electrician working on a machine to do that right now,' and certainly Jimi was bringing colour, and space sounds, into the heads of new-found German fans.

It was a record-breaking tour, and it showed that the Experience in Germany were making new inroads into a Europe they were soon to virtually own, musically.

Jimi and the group had played a few dates in Hamburg before, at the famous 'Star Club', birthplace of rock 'n' roll and the Beatles in Germany, so they were looking forward to playing Hamburg again, especially since it was the only place on the tour where they already had a tested following and reputation.

Noel Redding commented before they reached Hamburg that 'Berlin was nice—we caused quite a big scene there—but when we get to Hamburg it should be even better'. They caused a big scene in Frankfurt too, and succeeded in achieving that time-honoured accolade of rock groups—ejection from their hotel.

'It wasn't for any particular reason,' said Noel, 'it was just because they didn't like the look of us. And everyone stares at us all the time—in hotels, in the street. But the kids are great—they love us. The whole scene's so funny but we're going down like a bomb and that's all that matters.'

Mid-tour, Jimi added his own comments: 'The whole group is feeling shattered because of the tight schedule of the tour,' and because one night they had met up with Dave Dee Dozy Beaky Mick & Tich (remember them!), who at that time were one of Germany's top-selling acts. 'We looned around with them all night,' laughed Jimi, 'and we didn't get back to the hotel till 8 o'clock the next morning. We were so shattered we just sat down and had a nice pint of German beer. Wow!'

Noel's final comment was: 'It should all be a bit of a laugh.' No doubt he relished the prospect of outraging staid Swedes and disapproving Danes with the group's incredible clothes and hairstyles.

After converting, musically, as many German youths as came within earshot of the super magnetism of the Jimi Hendrix Experience, with its addictive doses of psychedelic sound ('Hip Hamburg cries Heil Hendrix', one headline had screamed) the group spread across Europe, popularity-wise, like a musical plague; and instead of bringing death, as the word plague generally implies, they brought a new musical life, a new era of space-age mind-blowing music which itself helped to usher in a new period of greater freedom of expression throughout Europe for the young. Jimi's hairstyle became one of the most popular and widely-imitated on the continent, until everywhere he went he would find boys and girls alike wearing hair like his own. Even wig manufacturers, realising there was a ready-made market created by Jimi's popularity, seized the opportunity successfully, selling nearly as many Hendrix wigs as Jimi was selling records.

The Experience flew straight on to Scandinavia for a whirlwind tour of Sweden, Denmark and Finland, adding, there, even more fans to their international collection, which by now amounted to a cult following of epidemic proportions.

The group returned to England on 28 May (1967) to find their album well on its way to being a smash hit. They did not, however, rest on their considerable laurels for long. The first week in June they were away again, this time for a two-week but four-country tour. It took them back to Germany (where they started out re-conquering Berlin) and then to Holland, Belgium and Italy.

After that, it was to be ... America. There were many spiritual forces at work pushing the destiny of Jimi Hendrix forward, and one casual event that had happened in the first few weeks of Jimi's residence in England was now, months later, to have repercussions that were to take him back across the Atlantic, this time in triumph.

The Beatles had caught Jimi's early act in the London clubs, and Paul McCartney had been especially impressed. Just as earlier he had given Jimi his ticket to the British hip-establishment scene by inviting him to star-studded parties, so now he proved instrumental in providing him with another and more far-reaching ticket to ride.

'Jimi Hendrix,' Paul announced, 'is a musical pioneer, a creative genius,' and decided to recommend this American abroad to the Selection Committee of the forthcoming Monterey Pop Festival back in America. 'It will not be a Festival,' he assured them, 'without Jimi Hendrix and the Experience.'

So everything was indeed in readiness for Jimi and the group to make their explosive entrance into America's burgeoning musical scene. At least, it was to be an 'entrance' for Noel Redding and Mitch Mitchell—for Hendrix himself, it was to be a *re*-entrance: the return of the prodigal.

CHAPTER FIVE

The return of the prodigal

Jimi told me how he had felt on the plane trip that sped him back to the United States for the début of the Experience and subsequent Monterey Pop Festival appearance in June '67:

'I felt as if I was coming back to reality after taking a tab of acid,' said Jimi. 'And for a few minutes I wondered if I had really been in England at all.'

When he touched down on American soil, that same feeling was still running around his head: 'Coming back to America was like coming down from a trip, really. But then I looked around and saw Bob Dylan's grandmother—meaning Mitch Mitchell: that was one of the names I enjoyed calling Mitch when we were on stage—and I knew everything must be real.'

He talked, too, of his feelings about checking through customs and into a hotel—all those initial hassles where the old prejudices might rear up again in the old American way.

'I knew we were going to get the super-search treatment when we went through customs,' Jimi told me. 'I don't think they were quite ready for us—me in my yellow silk pants and purple silk shirt and with my electric hair, and Noel and Mitch with their wild-coloured clothes and long hair. And indeed the US customs officials didn't disappoint. They took one look and you would have thought they had discovered the top three men on the FBI's Ten Most Wanted Men list. And by the time they were through searching us we almost thought we were them.'

They didn't find anything.

'We didn't carry anything in,' Jimi told me, laughing, 'because we knew we could get whatever we wanted right there in America!'

And the hotel hassles? 'Man,' said Jimi, 'we checked into this hotel right off 5th Avenue, and I knew by the way the desk clerk and the manager looked at us that this was a bad scene.

'It was one of those exclusive hotels where they spend a lot of bread in the lobbies to impress the people. It had carpet so thick you felt like you were walking on a cloud; mirrored halls and the whole trip. They were geared to cater to your every whim—for a price, of course. But not for cats like us, man. We lasted a day and a half.'

After that, he said, the predictable happened. Jimi had figured that the hotel management would decide that having rock musicians around might give the place a bad name and would, sooner or later, try an old familiar New York hotel trick. Sure enough, a phone call came through, very apologetic; there had been a mistake and they would have to give up their rooms because there was a reservation that had been made prior to theirs and there were no more rooms available. That was the standard polite way of telling them to get the hell out.

What really worried Jimi, in fact, was the feeling that maybe the hotel would prove a microcosm of America— that maybe he would be told to 'get the hell out' of American rock music.

Chas Chandler, after all, had taken Jimi to Britain to
launch him not only because that was familiar territory
for Chas to steer his managerial way around but also because
of Britain's greater receptivity to both new music and black
musicians. For Jimi to come to the Monterey Festival was
an attempt by a black musician to spearhead a new music
in a field almost totally dominated by white middle-class
groups and their white middle-class hippie audience
Hendrix didn't consider that as just another step in his
climb: he considered it a daring and hazardous risk, a brave
undertaking.

In America, black acts simply were not being booked on
the scope possible on the European concert scene—they
didn't have access to the really big halls and auditoriums.
And that meant they didn't have access to the really big
money which white artists were pulling in. The old blues
artists were allowed to die in harrowing poverty in their
homeland, and those who were helped were those lucky
enough to be 'discovered'—that is, re-discovered—by
European music researchers, who brought them to Britain
where they were able to perform again to appreciative
audiences. And the younger generation of black artists,
whose music was Soul and R & B, were rarely afforded the
opportunity to play outside of the small-audience networks
—the clubs and the few-and-far-between specialist black
theatres like the Apollo Theater in Harlem. Even in Europe,
a black artist was remarkably lucky to play in any bigger
forum than an R & B-orientated club or a cabaret venue or
small ballroom.

So Jimi was apprehensive. He was challenging the whole
economic pattern of black musicianship in America. Other
black artists simply did not command the kind of money
that he had begun to have a taste of in Europe. He had
become one of Europe's hottest acts; he had been welcomed
there with open arms and given his chance strictly on the

basis of his musical ability and talent—something he felt
he had been denied up till now in America because he was
black and because he was different. Now, as he saw very
plainly, in simple and practical terms, what he was doing
was returning to claim some of that Yankee Doodle Dollar
which he deserved and which was long overdue.

He was surprised when people recognised him in the
street in New York City: not people who had known him
before when we had played the Big Apple club-scene together, but people who, obviously, were aware of his
European reputation. He had thought no-one in the States
had heard of the Jimi Hendrix Experience, other than those
few who kept up with international sections of *Cashbox*
and *Bill-Board* and the other trade papers, in which rumours
had filtered through.

Nevertheless, the reputation of the Experience *had* preceded their arrival; the more knowledgeable fans of the rock
scene were aware of the name and the image, and were
waiting with marked anticipation to see the group in
action.

In addition, the American rights to the Experience's
records had been signed up by Reprise Records—the company set up by Frank Sinatra and then sold to the vast
Kinney group of companies (owners, also, of almost all the
parking lots in New York City). The advance paid by Reprise was reputedly in excess of 250,000 dollars. That is a
relatively small sum now, but in 1967 it was very big indeed.
Moreover, the advance orders placed by the stores for the
first album, *Are you Experienced?*, were enormous (one report even claimed a figure of a million copies).

So there was, whether it reassured Jimi himself or not,
a considerable amount of evidence to suggest that his
imminent American appearances would bring success and
expansion rather than rejection, failure or whatever
humiliation Jimi was scared of bringing down upon his

head. The 5th Avenue hotel was unlikely to prove typical of America.

In any event, from that hotel, Hendrix and his entourage checked into the more hospitable Gorham Hotel on West 55th Street between Avenue of the Americas and 7th Avenue. The Gorham catered for rock groups, who were always allocated rooms on the same floor in order to mini- mise the likelihood of their coming into contact with the 'straight' guests.

Once ensconced in his Gorham suite, Jimi got in touch with me and asked me to come over to meet Noel and Mitch and to have a long rap.

I walked into Jimi's room and found it full of groupies which fitted my picture of Jimi.

Noel and Mitch were very friendly but, I got the feeling, very shy. They were sort of open yet wary at the same time. It bugged me a little bit at the time, but I know now that they had a lot to be shy about. It was their first trip to America, and Jimi was proving none too easy to please— Mitch generally suffered in silence but Noel wouldn't do that, he flared up fast and slanged back at Jimi. So they had problems.

They had the small additional problem of it being their first experience also of American groupies—but even though it contributed to their shyness when I first met them that day in the hotel-room, they soon discovered that those par- ticular beautiful people were very into Englishmen.

I was very sensitive, I admit, to the signs of prosperity —the *atmosphere* of prosperity—in Jimi's room. He had this dynamite portable record-player, which was unbeliev- ably good and reeked of money, and he showed me all the far-out clothes he had brought over from England—great piles of silks and velvets, the likes of which I had personally never seen. America just didn't have clothes like that, and so to me, never having been to Britain, they seemed truly revolutionary in style.

'Hey, Bro',' he said to me, putting his hand over his mouth —an old habit he hadn't lost in England, 'I want you to listen to these demos of songs I'm going to record. I'm really getting into something now.' He said it as if nothing he'd already done had any value for him—as if this new stuff was the first time he'd ever been pleased with his work; yet to me, everything he'd ever played had been far out, all the way from the first time he'd picked on my guitar way back in that very different kind of hotel room in 1965.

He put one of the demos on the record-player and as ever, it was incredible music. I told him how much I liked it, commented on the marriage between the drums and guitar, and said how amazing I thought it was to get such a full sound from just three pieces. He seemed particularly pleased that I dug it, and relieved that I was being friendly.

The relief was mutual, and we both sensed that we could get a better vibe going between us again if we went down to the Village together, as we had done many many times before. Jimi was anxious to go buy a whole pile of the latest albums (Dylan, the Stones and the Beatles were his favourites, but there were also many records by lesser-known names which didn't get released in Britain that he was keen to catch up on) so we left Noel and Mitch and the chicks in his room and set off down the Gorham corridors.

Right then something happened which I thought very puzzling at the time. Jimi said: 'Wait a minute—I don't have any money, so I have to go get some from my manager. Come on and go with me while I pick up some money and then we can go to the record shops.' He knocked on his manager's door. It opened ever so slightly, as if his manager Mike Jeffries had secret company. At any rate, he didn't want to be disturbed.

Jimi asked him for some money, and I was shocked when

he told him that he couldn't give him any and that they'd talk about it later. I could see that Jimi was both embarrassed and angry at the same time. I asked him what kind of a financial arrangement he had with the people who were supposed to be looking after his interests.

'Well,' he said, 'they receive the money and take care of it for me, and whenever I need some, I just ask for it.' It didn't sound too good an idea in the context of what had just happened.

I asked him if he knew what they did with it after they collected it; he said he thought they put it in the bank for him. But he didn't know what bank, he had no bank book, and he had no idea how much money he was supposed to actually have in there. I said I'd never heard of an arrangement like that, and his answer was just that he thought he could trust them. Later, Jimi was to change his attitude to money quite considerably. Nearer the end of his tragically short career he was to become very money-conscious, and the embarrassed, vague Jimi Hendrix that I was commiserating with in the hotel corridor was to step down in favour of a far more financially shrewd and careful star. Even then, it was too late—Jimi never saw anything like the amount of money he earned. Chas Chandler was a straightforward guy, but he was to quit managing Hendrix because of his disagreements with Mike Jeffries; and in any case, Chandler was, like Brian Epstein, far more a creative manager than a businessman. Jeffries, on the other hand, was a businessman through and through, and it would be hard to say he was straightforward. And in the end, the great weight of financial tangles surrounding the Hendrix monies was never sorted out, because Mike Jeffries died in a plane crash the day before he was to give evidence in the case that was in progress and which, as a result of his death, was subsequently settled out of court.

But that is jumping ahead. Back there in that hotel corridor in June 1967, Jimi and I had to find him some spending money from somewhere. Ironically enough, I suggested that we should go round and see the man who was later to bring that court case—the man who had signed Jimi to a recording and management contract back in 1965: a contract which was still valid and which had been violated by Jimi's secret departure to England—Ed Chalpin. It was a crazy situation. There was Jimi, angry and humiliated because his new management wouldn't give him any money, and we decided that the best place to go get some money was from the manager Jimi had deserted when he had quit New York City without a word the year before.

I called Ed Chalpin and Jimi spoke to him on the phone and Ed told him we should come right over. We went over to Ed's studio and Ed gave Jimi some money, and all he said was that the three of us should have dinner together later that evening.

'After all,' said Ed quietly, 'there are some things we have to discuss.' He was pretty good about the whole thing.

So we agreed to have dinner with Ed Chalpin that night, and in the meantime Jimi and I went to the Colony Record Store, which was then located on the corner of 53rd Street and Broadway. (It has since moved to a larger place on 49th Street and Broadway.)

We were stopped in the street many times by people who wanted simply to shake his hand. Some of the people were guys who remembered him from before, when we were playing the clubs together—because it was only, after all, about a year earlier that we had been doing the rounds. But many people knew Jimi just from the advance publicity that the Experience had received, and many more just stared at him on account of the far-out clothes he was dressed in.

He was very pleased to find such a welcome on the streets —it allayed at least part of his apprehension about his forthcoming Monterey appearance. He leaned over to me at one point, as he was signing an autograph for two foxy young girls, and said, 'Things are a little different now! The foxes swarm round like bees for the honey!' I told him I didn't recall he was exactly short of admirers when we had played together in New York City before, but that it was true that nobody had stood in line for autographs before.

'Well I guess you got that right,' Jimi laughed.

We went on into the record store, where Jimi proceeded to buy what seemed like every album in sight. We hung around there a long time, listening to albums and talking about music. The vibe was great, it seemed to me. It was just as if Jimi had never been away, except that he was dressed so extraordinarily and he had acquired a habit of extravagance.

If anything, Jimi seemed even happier with our reunion than I was, and before the evening was through he told me that he was very anxious to record with me again. He told me that he thought we had really started getting into some heavy and groovy things before he went to England and he wanted to pick up where we had left off.

This, of course, was in complete contradiction to what he told the press about the recordings that were issued with the two of us performing together. To the press he claimed that they were all very old recordings and that he had little to do with them, and that indeed many consisted of scraps of tape from the cutting-room floor stuck together with much dishonest technical wizardry. He knew as well as I did that that was not true. The recordings we had made before included tracks cut within a few short months of his arrival in England, and those that we laid down during Jimi's first trip back to the USA were, of course, genuine 1967 Hendrix—made after *Hey Joe*, after *Purple Haze*, after the *Are you Experienced?* album: made, it is fair to say, at the height of Jimi's exploratory creative power.

I should add that I never blamed Jimi himself for what he said about all these recordings. He had his own management to appease, his own image to protect and his own recording career to structure. I understood the pressures and the reasons for his statements. Equally, I understood the hostility of his business machine to the release of the records we made together—though my sympathy did not extend to them as it did to Jimi himself. What I have never understood is the fashionable indifference and downright hostility of outside commentators, particularly among the music press, on whose part it shows little appreciation of Hendrix's musicianship. If they can happily subscribe to the falsehood that our *Ballad of Jimi* was a rip-off designed to cash in on Jimi's death, when in fact Jimi is playing all the instruments on the track except the drums; and if they can complacently dismiss our *Get that Feeling*, for instance, as being an old patched-together track, when in fact Jimi and I recorded it after our reunion dinner with Ed Chalpin that night in June 1967, then they show an astonishing lack of familiarity with Jimi's style and distinctive talent.

That is my position, and that is the real story. We returned from the Colony Record Store, had dinner with Ed Chalpin, and then went into his studio for the recording session which produced, among many tracks, *Get that Feeling*, which was the title track of the Capitol album released in early 1968.

The dinner was at a place called The Diner, which was open twenty-four hours a day and was located at the corner of 43rd Street and 11th Avenue in Manhattan. The Diner was frequented by a lot of the night people of New York—dancers, musicians, cab-drivers, hustlers, and ladies of the evening. It was a popular place with large booths, a bar, and an additional huge dining-room that catered for banquets, and its main attraction was that you could get a lunch in the middle of the night, a dinner at breakfast-time or a breakfast in the late afternoon. Any meal you wanted anytime.

Ed Chalpin told Jimi that all of us would have to go to court, because Jimi was still legally under contract to him. Jimi was quiet and talked quite openly about what had happened as he had understood it.

'The people that took me to England,' he said, 'told me that they had seen you. They said they'd seen you about it and straightened everything out. Because, you know, when they first approached me about going to England I told them that I had a legal contract that was still in effect.'

When Ed had talked some more, explaining things from his side, Jimi said OK, he understood, and he agreed that 'the matter will now have to be taken to court to be straightened out'.

Then he grinned at both of us and said: 'I don't care what the people that took me to England think, I'm going to continue recording with you and Curtis, Ed, because the three of us had a good scene. You as engineer, Ed, and Curtis and I out in the studio swinging.'

So we set up a recording session for that night, and as far as I was concerned it was a fantastic session. We really got it on and we recorded many titles, including *Get that Feeling*. And subsequently we recorded together two or three more times while Jimi was in New York City, because we both dug what we were into together.

The night I remember in particular was the night of Jimi's press party where all the critics finally got to see The Jimi Hendrix Experience.

It was ironic that the owner of the club where the Experience played its début engagement in the US was the same man who had owned Ondines, where the Jimi Hendrix Curtis Knight Band had been booked and had played that first time Chas Chandler had heard Jimi play. Bradley, his name was.

When the group came on stage they were greeted by tumultuous applause from the strange mixture of long-haired music magazine writers and a star-studded audience of pop stars and their freaked-out chicks in velvets and satins, and other record-company executives. It was a crowded, shoulder-to-shoulder and ass-to-ass situation in the club that night. A masher's paradise.

It was very hot in there, and with Jimi's powerful, driving performance, it got a lot hotter, and the audience thought it was mind-blowing. Like everyone else, I too was seeing the Experience in action for the first time, and I too thought the group was incredible; but knowing Jimi as I did, I could tell that he was far from happy with what was going down.

Jimi was always very conscientious and possessed with tremendous pride and concern about his performances, and being the versatile musician that he was, he could always detect the slightest mistake or deviation from a pre-arranged and carefully rehearsed rendition. I could tell by the expression on his face that he felt something was wrong, even though he was being extremely well received. Between numbers especially, he would turn round to Noel or Mitch and just with a glance convey a message of dissatisfaction. At times I was close enough to the stage to hear him mutter 'Come on! Get it together!' and 'Where were you on that last song? Wake up, man!'

Immediately after their encores, they rushed back to their dressing-room, and by the time I had pushed my way in there, through the sweating, sweltering crowd, there was Jimi standing up like a General berating his troops over a costly battlefield disaster. He made it very clear, in no uncertain terms, just how far from happy with their American début he had been.

Mitch didn't have much to say; he just sort of sat there with his head down, sweating profusely and not having much success trying to dry off with a towel. The more he wiped, the more the sweat came, partly because he had not yet unwound from the rigours of his extraordinary drumming, and partly because a crowd of people had pushed their way into the tiny room, bringing their own smells and sweat with them and adding to the uptight atmosphere that already prevailed. While Mitch just sat there wiping away at his glistening body, Noel Redding, very much in contrast, was matching Jimi almost word for word in a confrontation that I thought might any minute come to physical blows. Then suddenly, with one last violent outburst from both of them, they seemed to declare a mutual truce. They stood there glaring at each other while everyone else stared at them both.

Jimi was uptight because Noel had deviated from the bass pattern that Jimi had taught him to play—something which on no account was he supposed to have changed. Noel said he didn't mind being shown a particular bass line but he did *not* like being told exactly what he *had* to play.

This recurrent difference of opinion was to lead to deeper and more irresolvable disharmony within the band as they climbed even further towards the dizzy heights of their much-deserved success. Perhaps Noel Redding had already realised that the lack of communication in terms of creating song arrangements together would inevitably result in the break-up of the group. Perhaps that was why Noel had acquired a reputation as the cautious, conservative one in the group—the one who not only looked after his earnings carefully but never spent one penny more than was absolutely necessary to survive.

Mitch Mitchell, on the other hand, was less frustrated, more complacent about the situation, and seemed more content to let Jimi have his way. The very fact that he had a kind of free-form drumming style meant, of course, that he had more independence in the group than Noel; but in any case I think Mitch's theory was that it was better to be a member of a winning team than to be, despite a greater musical freedom, on the outside looking in at someone else's beautiful scene.

Anyway, by the time the group's début that night was over, and they had finished in the dressing-room, it was about

2.30 in the morning—and that was when Jimi decided we should do another recording session. He wanted to wake up Ed Chalpin and go back into the studio. He said there were some musical ideas that had come to him that day which he wanted to record with me.

So, still running at high-energy level after two dynamite sets played for all the writers and music businessmen, Jimi got into my car and we went to Ed Chalpin's apartment and got him out of bed. He opened up the studio and with him acting again as engineer, Jimi and I spent the rest of the night recording.

After we finished, we went onto the Scene, which at that time was one of the favourite places where Jimi and I liked to go and jam, and saw the morning in from the club's basement, where you were always likely to see any pop star who was visiting the city. The club was in a neighbourhood where junkies, pickpockets and whores walked the streets: a poor neighbourhood, but one whose atmosphere was not unfamiliar to the Jimi Hendrix I had first met, hard-up and unknown, in 1965. Jimi had indeed come home.

But from there, Jimi went on, with the Experience, to play some more standing-room-only gigs across the USA, and then came in triumph to the Monterey Pop Festival.

Monterey was the first of the big pop festivals—a logical offspin/equivalent of the Newport festivals of jazz and folk music. It was held 16-18 July 1967, and featured an unparalleled weekend of rock giants performing from morning until the midnight curfew that was agreed upon by the organisers and the local police. The stars included Simon & Garfunkel, The Who, the Buffalo Springfield, Lou Rawls, Ravi Shankar, the Mamas and the Papas, and Otis Redding.

Otis Redding was in the position discussed earlier in this chapter : like Jimi he was black, and it was no sure thing that he would 'fit in' with the rest of the acts. And indeed, appearing in a 'straight' shiny suit, he did look a little incongruous. But he was one of the first acts to get the 50,000 + audience up and dancing and surging towards the stage in waves of enthusiasm. They loved him, and they embraced his soul music. It was his pinnacle of success, though he didn't have long to enjoy it. He died in a plane crash when he was twenty-six years old.

Otis Redding epitomised the 1960s soul artist, the inheritor of the progress made by an older generation of men like Joe Turner and Fats Domino, who were in turn the inheritors of the blues. In this sense, Otis Redding was a traditional artist. Jimi Hendrix, on the other hand, though he drew on and was much influenced by the blues, was not a traditional artist— was not so much an upholder, like Redding, but a genuine boundary-leaping innovator.

When the Jimi Hendrix Experience emerged onstage at Monterey, they ushered in the psychedelic era with walls of amplifiers, the likes of which had never been experienced or seen together before in America, and with clothes that seemed truly revolutionary. The very sight of them as they were announced gave a vividly colourful hint of momentousness, but it was when they began to play that they really took off.

They took their audience on a space flight, the Hendrix guitar screaming, the group rolling and thundering, and the whole impact enhanced by Jimi's sensual movements and his intimacy with his guitar, which brought girls in the huge crowd screaming to their feet in sexual adulation, in proportions unknown since the early days of Elvis Presley's first across-the-nation concerts. Indeed, after the Monterey Festival, some journalists dubbed him 'The new Elvis of Rock' and 'A Black Sexual Phenomenon'. (They ignored, with such labels, the creativity of his music.)

Jimi did indeed conquer Monterey. He was, literally, a howling success.

Eric Burdon told me he had seen the performance and remembered it like this:

'It was great, performance-wise. Man, when Otis Redding was on—I think it was Otis Redding, somebody heavy was on the stage—I told these kids sitting around me in the audience, "Wait until you see Jimi Hendrix," I said. "He's this new guitar player." And they were sitting near and they passed me a joint and I smoked a joint with them and they moved about twenty rows further down from where I was. And when Jimi came on, in about the middle of the third number, these three heads popped up and they turned around and they said: "Yes. We see what you mean! You're right." '

Afterwards, Jimi told me: 'Man, when I stepped out on that stage in my black military jacket with the gold braids, with all those foxes in the audience, I decided I would make love to all of them with my guitar, and I know that they had to feel it because I felt it.'

Pete Townshend didn't think Jimi went down quite so fantastically well, but as he admitted to me, his view was a little bit jaundiced by jealousy. He told me:

'When we worked with Jimi on that Monterey thing, I started to realise what a curse he was, he being on our label and having connections through our manager. Believe it or not, he was our fucking back-up group, so we used to have to follow this bastard on the stage, and try and whip up some enthusiasm after he'd done it all. I never wanted to play. I just used to stand in the wings, and because I sorta went through it with him, I felt I'd done my gig anyway, and had to go on and do it again. We just had to live with the fact that he was going to be kicking around for a while, until he finally did explode in the way that he was always meant to.

'When we arrived at Monterey, Jimi was just as horrified as I, to see that we were on the same day, and they put the two

acts back to back, so he said to me, "Listen I'm not following
your band", and I said, "I'm not following you," if you see
what I mean. Anyway, I persuaded Jimi to let us go on first,
because I told him that the way I figured it, the kind of guitar
smashing thing we were gonna get into was, you know,
we were having to pull out a lot of the old tricks, for
Monterey was a big sort of showcase for us, and it was for
Jimi too, because that was his jumping off point.

'So we smashed up the guitar and all this. Then Jimi came
on and did his thing and, of course, he blew everyone's mind
to begin with. Then, at the end, when he smashed his gear up,
the audience were numb, you know, it was very weird, they
couldn't work it out.

'I was in the audience, watching, and it threw me, because,
of course, every time I've seen him in England, there had
been a huge ovation at the end, and when we did it the first
time, we smashed all the equipment up, and feedback, and
God knows what. The crowd didn't quite know how to take
it, and then they reacted in claps. When he did it, they
thought the whole world had gone mad. He set light to his
pissing guitar. He poured lighter fuel all over it and set light
to it, and they couldn't believe it was happening. Afterwards,
relationships weren't too good between Jimi and me, because
I think he was sort of disturbed by the whole thing. I
don't think he felt he had big enough equipment, or something.'

Yet despite Townshend's impressions, Jimi was actually far
from unhappy about the concert.

He told me, 'I set my guitar on fire at the Monterey Pop
Festival because it had given all it could give—it had said
all there was to say and it was sent out in a blaze of glory'
(again, literally) 'as a requiem for the immortal statement it
had made that night for me.' Undoubtedly he was pleased
with the group's performance *that* night, and—as his
remarks suggest—particularly pleased with his own virtuoso

performance. As usual, he felt he played his best when he was nicely stoned.

'You know,' he told me, 'some fox brought me this incredible grass, man. She said she got it from someone who got it in Mexico—and it was nice; nice. Plus I also had some nice coke, so I was really mellow when I went on stage.'

'Mellow', of course, was far from how he appeared. Added to the dynamism that was an intrinsic part of Jimi's stage-act, there was, by the time of the Monterey appearance, an undeniable urgency in everything that Jimi did—as if he felt he might have somehow been behind schedule in fulfilling his destiny.

Whether or not that was the case, Monterey undoubtedly did everything Jimi's management had hoped it would, giving him a real accelerative boost. Jimi became an overnight superstar, an underground hero, and posters began to appear in every head shop all across the United States. Coast to coast, everyone began to wear the extravagant Hendrix hair-style, plus an imitative regalia of medals and chains around their necks. He had earned the first of the really big fees to which he could from now on lay claim. And, more important still to Jimi himself, the adulation that came out of the Monterey gig meant that there was a real spiritual gain. Jimi could feel, from this point on, that he could really communicate with his audience, so they would be more receptive to his message of love and peace.

He had been beautifully sincere—almost apologetic—in his conversations with the audience between songs: as if he wanted every person there to know that he was musically talking directly to them. As Mitch Mitchell said, 'You could see the beauty of the injecting of his feelings from his head ... into his fingers and then into his guitar; and you could see the audience feel the beautiful effects of his soul.'

The impact he made on American music that night was, in other words, profound. As one of the newspapers phrased it, 'The Jimi Hendrix Experience ... graduated from rumour to legend.'

Hendrix caught the ear of another 'legend', too—the irascible Bill Graham, owner of the Fillmore West in San Francisco and the Fillmore East in New York City, and the father of the stoned West Coast concert scene. Graham wanted Hendrix to play the Fillmores, which were the most prestigious rock venues around at that time, and would have been, indeed, the logical follow-through opportunities after Monterey.

It wasn't possible, however. Jimi wanted to do it, Chas Chandler wanted to do it, Noel and Mitch wanted to do it, and Bill Graham wanted to do it. But Mike Jeffries had signed the Experience for a tour with teenybop idols The Monkees, and no gaps were available for any Fillmore appearances. (When the group *did* get around to their first Fillmore West concert, a couple of months later, they were on the same bill as Jefferson Airplane. The Experience got such a wild reception that the Airplane came on nervous and diffident, and quit ahead of time. The Experience then returned to the stage and played out the end of the concert, receiving in consequence a 2,000-dollar bonus from a delighted Bill Graham.)

This signing of the Experience to a tour with The Monkees began the really serious split between Chas Chandler and Mike Jeffries. Eric Burdon, who had been brought to London from Newcastle by Mike Jeffries in the early days of the British beat-group boom in the 1960s, says in the interview I had with him that it was Chas Chandler who booked Hendrix on the Monkees tour knowing that he would be thrown off it because of 'obscenity' and that the publicity gained from that would be invaluable. What Jimi himself told me contradicts that. What actually happened was that Jeffries booked him on the tour and Chandler was, like Jimi himself, very much opposed to, and angry at, this *fait accompli* which Jeffries had finalised without consulting the others; but that indeed it was Chas Chandler who turned it to Hendrix's advantage by setting up the stories about the shocked disapproval of the Daughters of the American Revolution, so that the group could quit the Monkees tour as if they *had* been thrown off it and could indeed then capitalise on the publicity that ensued.

So that was what happened—and was one of the significant contributing factors to Chas Chandler's eventually selling his 50 per cent interest in Jimi Hendrix to Mike Jeffries, so that Jeffries emerged as sole manager except insofar as the lawsuits were floating around between Jeffries and Ed Chalpin. The Jimi Hendrix Experience began an across-the-nation tour of America on the same bill as The Monkees, idols of the eleven-to-thirteen-year-olds of clean suburban America.

'Yeah,' Jimi told me, 'it was Mike Jeffries that arranged for that stupid tour with The Monkees. That wasn't our kind of scene and he should have known that—but what could I do? He booked it, so I had to play; but the people who came to hear The Monkees' bubble-gum music didn't even know what we were doing. I was glad when we got thrown off the tour. I felt a little bit embarrassed but I was still glad to be out of that trap.'

It certainly must have been an incongruous evening for anyone who caught the Monkees-Hendrix tour. As Lilian Roxon described the situation, in her book *Rock Encyclopaedia* (Grosset and Dunlap 1969),

'... It was the summer of 1967 and the Monkees tour, and no mother who had taken her little apple-cheeked daughter to shriek over Pete, Mike, Mickey and Davey was ready for what Hendrix got into that hot night out at the Forest Hills Stadium. Lyne Randell, who was little and blonde and wholesome, had just sung her numbers in her sequined jump suit. It was a bit daring, *Going out of my head*, and Mom got very protective about that. But wait. That was nothing. On stage now with that insolent saunter came The Jimi Hendrix Experience. Three huge frizzy dandelion heads. Three decadent Regency rakes. Amplifiers turned up to infinity. And now the star, like Christ between his two thieves, black hair flying from his head in electric fright, doing things to his guitar so passionate, so concentrated and so intense that anyone with half decent manners had to look away. And that was the way the act began, not ended. By the time it was over he had lapped and nuzzled his guitar with his lips and tongue, caressed it with his inner thighs, jabbed at it with a series of powerful pelvic thrusts. Even the little girls who'd come to see the Monkees understood what this was about.'

The furore was inevitable, and Chas Chandler utilised it to the full, so that the Jimi Hendrix Experience had to drop out of the remaining dates for which they'd been signed. In point of fact, the reality was that Chandler wanted Hendrix to drop out, and had managed to concoct the ideal solution. They got let out of the commitment they had been let in for by Jeffries; and thus they were free to embark on their own equivalent of the tour : a series of sell-out concert dates elsewhere in the USA.

The first of these concerts was under the auspices of the Premiere Talent Agency of New York (and not, as often reported, sponsored by Schaefer Beer) and was held in the city's Central Park, with the Experience topping a bill that also featured the Young Rascals, of *Grooving* fame. After Central Park, there were several more lucrative engagements, including the overdue performance at Bill Graham's Fillmore West, before Jimi and the others flew back to Britain.

They were back in Britain by late August, for two performances at London's latest rock venue, the Savile Theatre

—though in the event, the second show was cancelled after the news had spread through the music business that Brian Epstein, creative manager and mentor of the Beatles, had been found dead.

Hendrix did another 'downer' concert in London nearer the end of the year, when he featured in the Christmas On Earth Concert at Olympia. It was a fine concert but a financial flop, and the sour taste of that lingered.

It all seemed to augur badly for the kind of forums for live music which Jimi himself communicated best in and wanted to see doing well. 'I felt really bad when they told me that Brian Epstein had died,' Jimi told me. 'He was a very young and progressive cat and he did so much for the Beatles.' More especially, Jimi was depressed because of what it meant for the London music scene: 'I feel that he is a great loss to all of us,' said Jimi, 'because he was trying to get a string of rock theatres together where groups could perform, and that would have helped everybody.'

Nevertheless, for Jimi Hendrix and his group, it had been a good year. And to round it off jubilantly, the Experience was voted 3rd Most Popular Group in Britain by the readers of *Melody Maker* magazine, and Hendrix got the Musician of the Year Award from both *Melody Maker* and *Disc* magazines.

CHAPTER SIX

Love and confusion

The recording sessions which Hendrix and the Experience had worked through in the summer of 1967 produced the next album, *Axis: Bold as Love*, which was released in March 1968—but by then Jimi had developed so much that the album seemed to him very much past history. And besides, a lot had happened by the time March came around.

In January, the group returned to Sweden. Their previous appearance there, in May '67, had been brief, but even before his arrival this second time around, Jimi was known and idolised by every flower-child in the land. His posters were a head-shop *must*, and adorned the walls of most of the hip people in Sweden's cities; and his record-sales in Sweden had been phenomenal. He was assured of a frenzied and demonstrative welcome.

Nevertheless, Hendrix was far from happy. There was turmoil raging in his head. At times, off-stage, he remained the gentle, super-sensitive person he had always been; at other times, he would suddenly become violent—lashing out mentally and physically—to a degree that was almost frightening.

Many different people remarked upon his changeability.

As Eric Burdon, for instance, told me:

'Jimi had these extreme opposites in character. Very much day and night. Very schizophrenic—dual personality. But then to some extent, everybody is, in the music business. Jimi was just an extremist.'

And if Jimi was growing more and more mixed-up, he was also feeling increasingly lonely. Quite by coincidence, I met a girl in the Speakeasy in London who had lived in Gothenburg in Sweden and had seen Hendrix back then in January '68, and whose story of their encounter shows by its very brevity and inconclusiveness, the desperate extent of Jimi's aloneness at that time.

'My girl-friends and I,' she told me, 'saw in the paper that the Jimi Hendrix Experience was in town, and we were all walking down the street discussing where they might be staying. I said I was sure Hendrix would be at the Hotel Opelan. And just then, this big car drove up and stopped; somebody stuck their head out of the window and asked us if we'd come to this Hotel Opelan to have a drink with them. We realised then that it was the Experience, so we went. We went to the hotel and in the bar, Jimi was there waiting.

'We had a few drinks with them and they were very nice; but we decided it was time to go when they invited us upstairs to their rooms.'

So there was Hendrix on 3 January 1968, a superstar returned in triumph to Sweden, failing to make it with a couple of ingenuous local girls, after sending a car out to pick them up in the street for him.

The next day, he smashed his hotel-room to smithereens.

When I asked him, next time I saw him again in New York, what had happened, he explained it like this:

'Man, we arrived in Sweden for the gigs and I was really looking forward to getting some sleep, and I thought all the reservations for our hotel had been made, because all of that is usually taken care of in advance. But I found out when we arrived that we had been refused reservations in about twenty hotels.' Smiling as he thought back over some of his more chaotic exploits, Jimi added : 'I couldn't for the life of me understand why !'

'But anyway,' he went on, 'we finally got rooms in this one hotel, and with all the confusion, I felt like getting high so I could get my head together. Then that night—I can't remember what time it was—I was so spaced, and Noel and I got into another one of our many hassles; but this one was a little heavier than most of the others, and as near as I can remember, we even swung a few punches at each other. Well, the next thing I remember, I woke up next morning in jail. And'—smiling again—'one thing I can tell you is that Swedish jails are not nearly as nice as Swedish girls.'

Other guests in the hotel said that someone was playing drums and guitar in Hendrix's room and then they started hearing screams, and these screams went on almost throughout the night. What they'd heard was Jimi's vicious row with Noel Redding, followed by his screams of spaced-out frustration as he smashed up everything in sight inside his room. The Swedish papers, when they got hold of the story, said the bill for damages was way over £400.

The police were called in to quell the disturbance, and it took three men to hold Jimi down, and a lot of time to calm him down. He was taken to the hospital under police guard; his hand was stitched where he had gashed it badly; he was taken back from the hospital, his passport was impounded, and he was thrown in jail.

When Chas Chandler saw him next morning, dishevelled and still spaced-out, sitting on the floor of his cell, he said, a little despairingly, 'What happened?'

'I can't remember,' said Jimi. 'Are you sure it wasn't just me dreaming?'

Chandler sprung him—paying damages, smoothing things over with the police and the other authorities—though whether the passport was retained until the end of the tour, or returned straight away, isn't clear.

Jimi, being Jimi, continued his tour as if nothing had happened, coping somehow with the difficulties and pain of playing with his stitched-up hand. But the altercation between him and Noel Redding, though seemingly forgotten by Jimi—at least on the surface—was far from forgotten or forgiven underneath; and that, along with Noel's creative frustration, their deep differences of opinion over recording technique, and Jimi's general discontents, was to contribute significantly to the feeling that the break-up of the group was inevitable.

In the latter part of January, Jimi and The Experience made their second return tour of America—a tour scheduled for approximately two months—this time headlining the bill, and accompanied by the Animals, the Soft Machine and Eire Apparent. There was none of the jealousy and aggro between the different acts on the tour, this time, that had beleaguered Hendrix in the past—and in fact he became sufficiently friendly with, and impressed by, Eire Apparent, that the following year, 1969, he acted as their producer for their record *Sunrise*.

But the tour did little to alleviate Jimi's dissatisfactions with the way things were going for him. By the time the tour reached the Anaheim Convention Hall, California, in February, he was no longer able to perform in the way that the public expected of him. 'They want me to be a monkey on the stage,' he said, and he couldn't do it any longer. The tickets for the concert there had been sold, as had become the norm, within hours of going on sale, and he came on stage to a capacity crowd. He played his music, but without any of the visual antics, the wild-man gimmickry, that had been his trade-mark. The crowd was disappointed, and he was heavily criticised for 'not bothering' by both the fans and the critics.

They didn't appreciate that he had felt torn long enough between his duty to please his audiences and his duty to himself and his deep longings that his music should stand up and be accepted for itself alone, without the accompanying stage routines for which he had become so famous. Neither did the audience or critics understand that it was tearing him apart in another sense too—because it meant him having to succumb to mechanical repetition in his act.

'Pop slavery,' Jimi called it, and told me: 'That's the trouble with this fucking business—people see where they can make fast bread, and they have you up there being a slave to the public. They keep you doing the same thing until you are exhausted. That's why groups break up—they get worn out.'

Jimi told me too that by the time they had reached the end of this American tour, he had realised that he needed a new musical direction, that there were so many things on his mind, things he wanted to do—like build his dream recording studio—and that at the same time, business pressures were getting heavier.

The tour was hectic, chaotic and—except in terms of Jimi's own satisfaction—highly successful. There had even been mini-riots and near-riots, when thousands of dollars' worth of counterfeit concert tickets were circulated, so that many Hendrix fans who turned up at his concerts were turned away, and ran wild in the streets around the theatres. Jimi didn't dig what was happening at all.

As far as he was concerned, only the girl situation was good—and even here, Jimi seemed to be screwing as a way of venting his anger—a way of hitting back at the Establishment. Everywhere he turned, he was getting 'young tender ones', as he used to call them. He was getting so much pussy, he told me, that he was almost living on it; 'Pussy for breakfast, dinner and supper.'

(I remember Eric Burdon saying to me:

'Jimi was so fascinated by women; so fascinated by the beauty of chicks. I think that's why I related to him so well, because he was into the things *inwardly*. Like, you won't understand how some chicks can be evil. So you have to examine the evil by getting close, next to the evil. The evil rubs off on you. Before you know where you are, you end up beating, beating, beating up on somebody's head, when really you shouldn't—or really you should, maybe: I don't know. It's just one of those trips you have to take. And Jimi was into all kinds of trips, man. You've got to be, as a creative artist, or you give up.')

Jimi seemed to get a particular kick out of the fact that most of the parents of the girls he was going through would have really flipped out if they had known that he was fucking their precious little daughters; and he saw those parents as being, in some general way, the enemy he was up against.

Yet even these 'young tender ones' were beginning to pall. Jimi told me:

'I would many times be just falling asleep from some all-night orgy and I would hear a gentle knock on my door; I'd stagger to the door naked and peep out, and there would be some sexy, cute little thing standing there, and she would ask if she could come in, and most of the time I'd say yes. But sometimes I would come in and the chicks somehow managed to get in the room and they would be waiting in bed for me when I didn't feel like being bothered, and I'd just get the roadies to throw them out.'

Later in February, the Experience took a break from America and flew to Paris for a return concert—going back to the Olympia Theatre where they had played their first-ever European gig, at Johnny Halliday's invitation, in December 1966. This time, they received the kind of welcome usually reserved for Presidents.

From Paris, they went back to New York, where Jimi

again came to see me and brought me up to date on what was happening. It seemed to me, that time around, that Jimi had changed—or, at any rate, was changing. I could see that the pressures of being a pop idol were taking their toll.

We talked about the fact that Jimi had lost a lot of weight, and he said, 'Well, I haven't been having much of an appetite lately; I've been getting stoned a lot. I just don't seem to remember to eat.'

He came with me down to a new soul-food restaurant that had opened up on 26th Street and 3rd Avenue (the same restaurant, by coincidence, where, shortly after Jimi's death, I bumped into Captain Beefheart, whose comments on Jimi's genius are included later in this book). So that night, at least, Jimi ate well.

He was very much looking forward, he said, to getting back to Seattle.

'Some time during this tour,' he mused. 'I haven't been back since I left to join the paratroopers, and I'll be glad to see everyone. I know they never thought I would make it, but I told them a long time ago that someday I would be famous. They didn't believe me!'

Jimi was a complex person. Gentle, but with a violent streak. Extrovert in his dress, but shy at the same time. Getting a kick—to begin with, anyway—out of his wild-man black stud image, yet wanting people's attention to be focused on his music alone. And as we sat together in that restaurant in the cold New York February of 1968, another paradox was obvious. That is, that on the one hand he was growing more and more to rely on old friends and to try for something approaching the old, simpler life he had enjoyed with them in the past; and on the other hand he was also growing more and more into the role of superstar—money-conscious superstar.

And this last was a noticeable change. No more vagueness about how much he was earning, where it was banked, or how it was distributed. This time around, he knew all about it, and told me with relish all the huge fees he was pulling in from his concert appearances and the massive royalties from his record sales.

Yet underneath, Jimi remained indifferent to money. Prior to the initial UK and European acceptance of the Experience, I don't think that even in his wildest imaginings Jimi thought he would ever be receiving such great sums of money. Even though he always seemed to feel that he would one day be a star, I don't think that he had ever thought realistically about the financial side of it, beyond a casual assumption that stardom would make him a Have instead of a Have Not.

By the time of this second American tour, Jimi realised that he—*his* talent—was largely responsible for the fabulous sums of money the group was pulling in, and he had started to notice the details of how it was split between them (50 per cent to Jimi, 25 per cent split between Mitch and Noel, and the other 25 per cent for the management) and how much each concert earned them. (It was, at that time, between 20,000 and 80,000 dollars per night's performance —and in fact at one place in the States, they received the incredible sum of 100,000 dollars for one forty-five-minute show.)

Jimi was aware of it all now; yet his indifference persisted in the way he spent it. He was truly one of the big spenders. He spent money extravagantly, casually, nonchalantly. On his slightest whim he would pick up bar and dinner tabs for great arrays of people. Kathy had unlimited credit at the Speakeasy in London, with Jimi paying her bills and never questioning the amount he was being charged. On one occasion, a girl he had never seen before came up to him at the Speakeasy and told me she needed some money to have her teeth fixed; Jimi gave her £300. Another time, he casually handed over 3,000 dollars to two girls he scarcely knew in California, so that they could 'go shopping'.

When Chas Chandler had been trying to get Hendrix launched in the early days, he had really put his money where his mouth was, as the old phrase has it, right down to selling his guitars—all of them, even his last bass guitar—in order that Jimi and he could survive long enough to get it all together. Now, in dramatic contrast, Jimi would some-times buy nine guitars at a time—and then smash them all up in one week and go out and buy ten or twelve more. At one period, he insisted on travelling with thirteen or four-teen of them, plus a massive assortment of other rock tech-nology—wah-wah pedals, fuzz-tone boxes, a warehouse-sized selection of spare parts, and various other devices that had been specially made for him at enormous expense.

In a sense, then, his new-found knowledgeability about his income was of no use to him whatever—because he never kept any proper records of his *out*goings. I suppose in some ways he was like the legendary Robin Hood: he could have been a millionaire several times over, but he spent so much and gave so much away, concentrating on his music instead of his bread. And in some ways, no doubt, that was a good thing. Yet it meant that many, many people ripped him off, and that a lot of money that was intended to go to deserving places didn't get there. He had, for instance, intended to give a considerable amount of money to his parents; but when I saw Jimi's father and step-mother in New York City shortly after his death, they told me that they had received nothing from his estate. They told me they could barely afford to pay their rent at that time, and so when someone stole Jimi's gravestone—the ultimate rip-off—they did not have the money to replace it.

At any rate, there was certainly some question as to whether Jimi had ever received all that was due to him.

But if, back then in that soul-food restaurant, Jimi was talking about his money, he was also, as ever, talking far more earnestly about his music, and about his spiritual destiny. I had always been fascinated by his beliefs and ideas about the world of the spirit, but this time, it seemed altogether more complicated a subject—more difficult for him to explain, and, I admit, more difficult for me to follow.

There was no revisit to Ed Chalpin's studios this time, and Jimi left New York to continue his gruelling, backbreaking tour. From New York, the Experience went to San Francisco, Texas, Arizona—and all the way up to Canada, where, the following year, he was to be busted on a drugs charge at Toronto International Airport.

But that is rushing ahead again, and must be left to the next chapter of this book.

The American tour continued—fifty-four concerts in forty-seven days, including an appearance on a bill shared with Frank Zappa and the Mothers of Invention in Miami. Jimi, of course, was especially keen on festivals, and remained so right to the end of his tragically guillotined career. Monterey, back in June 1967, had touched off his enchantment, and he never lost it. He had planned, following the US tour, to appear at a six-day pop 'n' jazz festival in Palma, Majorca, called 'Musica '68'—but to his disappointment, as much as that of the fans, the whole project was cancelled due to lack of capital on the part of the organisers.

When this fell through, Jimi and the Experience were still ploughing through their tour, with Hendrix himself getting more and more deeply unhappy about the whole thing. It was too demanding a schedule; there was the continual tug-of-war between the audiences' expectations of a strongly visual performance and Jimi's own desire to just play the music for the music's sake; and there was an accelerating deterioration of all the relationships Jimi was dependent on. Deterioration of trust and goodwill between Jimi and Noel (a seriously harmful situation as early as the beginning of January, as we have seen), and even between Jimi and Mitch. These divisions within the group were a terrible day-by-day strain on all three of them, but perhaps Jimi felt more deeply uneasy about the situation between himself and the management. He had told me himself, in New York, that he had begun to distrust the people who were handling his business, even though he admitted that they had done a lot for him. He had begun to realise more keenly that he had done a lot for them.

But at any rate, in May '68, Jimi did get back to Seattle. He was met at the airport by his father and by his younger brother, Leon, who is also a guitarist and by his step-mother, a lovely Japanese lady, whom Jimi had never met before.

As Jimi recalled this Seattle visit, 'I met my family and we were happy for a change. We enjoyed it. And I went to Garfield High School, where they kicked me out when I was sixteen, and I did a concert for the kids there. Just me. I played with the school band in the gymnasium! The only thing wrong with it was that it was at 8 o'clock in the morning. They cancelled first class to listen to me.'

Jimi was also scheduled to receive a highly prized honour, the Keys to the City; but the original date for the presentation clashed with a national holiday, and so it had to be postponed until November.

Jimi's comment, in any case, was that 'the only keys I thought I'd be involved with in Seattle were the keys to the jail'!

He did receive, for what it was worth, an honorary diploma from Garfield High. But what Seattle revisited did for Jimi, however, was really nothing to do with awards or presentations. What was really good was that Jimi got back among real people. It gave him the chance to come back to reality—to see once again the humble surroundings he had come from, and to have contact with genuine people not caught up in the maddening race of plasticity.

That is how he felt about it, and it was obviously true. Jimi returning home was like the re-charging of a battery, so that it might have a longer life. *He* was able to recharge his own long-overworked high-energy batteries: or, to change the metaphor, to drink up some fresh sap from his real roots.

If all this sounds as if Jimi was in many kinds of trouble, and as if 1968 was not a good year for him, it should be remembered that that was only the private side of the golden coin. In 1969, Jimi was indeed to have a bad year—his private difficulties affecting his career and his creativity to a serious and all-embracing extent, as we shall see. But in terms of his popularity, his public activity and achievement, 1968 was in fact Jimi's peak year. He was lauded and fêted, his records were selling phenomenally well, and his musical output seemed stronger and more innovative than even his staunchest early fans could have dared to hope or expect. In spite of the toned-down visuals, and his own fears about whether his music could be accepted in its own right, everybody loved him, fans and critics alike. Moreover, he had earned more admiration from other musicians than any other artist in rock music, with the one single exception of Bob Dylan.

Certainly, the record sales were booming. When the album *Get that Feeling—Jimi Hendrix Plays and Curtis Knight Sings* had been released in the USA in December 1967, *Cash Box*, the music trade paper, had reviewed it as follows:

'Jimi Hendrix shows off a scintillating guitar on this powerful LP, and Curtis Knight's hard-driving, funky vocals bristle with energy. The title track is particularly rousing ... This set should stir up considerable consumer reaction.'

It stirred up enough to make the album charts. When Jimi and I were rapping together again in February '68, the album was Number 45 in the *Cash Box* charts; and by the time Jimi was back with his folks in Seattle in May, the album was released in Britain, on London Records, and was in the UK album-charts at Number 39 by the end of the month.

By that time too, Track Records had issued a compilation album culled from Jimi's earlier hit albums and called *Smash Hits*. This entered the British album charts at Number 21, and by the first week of June it was in the Number 4 slot.

Meanwhile, the thirty-minute colour-TV film which John Marshall had made about Jimi—*The Jimi Hendrix Experience at the Savile Theatre*, 1967—had been previewed for international music industry executives at the Montreux Festival. It made, according to *Rolling Stone* magazine, a 'tremendous impact' and was immediately sold for transmission in Scandinavia, Holland, Finland and even Czechoslovakia and Poland. And by June '68, negotiations were underway for its transmission also in Germany, Japan and the USA.

By June, too, the Experience had fulfilled their massive American concert commitments, and Jimi was able to spend some time on the musical experiments which he had been so keen to get down to. He stayed in America, and spent most of the early part of the summer writing and composing new material, taping himself constantly, and assessing the results assiduously, and getting a great deal of pleasure, too, out of jamming with other stars and musicians. Buddy Miles, Mike Bloomfield, Jim Morrison, Stevie Winwood, Al Kooper, Johnny Winter, Dave Mason and Jack Casady were among them.

An interesting hint of all this renewed energy and behind-the-scenes activity was provided by a letter to *Rolling Stone* magazine by a New York musician called Paul Caruso, which was published on 22 June and reported that:

'Hendrix has done masses of jamming on the east coast

during March. He played with all from Mike Bloomfield to Jim Morrison. Jimi bought a four-track stereo tape-recorder and has been taping all his jam-sessions for future reference. Jimi is using various different musicians on his forthcoming triple-album, to be released when ready. I've played harp on a number called *My Friend* ... and made some bar-room noises with Steve Stills and Kenny of the Fugs ...'

(Some of the 'triple-album' referred to in Caruso's letter was to emerge towards the end of the year as the *Electric Ladyland* double-album. And not only were many of the musicians mentioned above on that album, when it surfaced, but Hendrix also played on one track of the *False Start* album by Love, and on one track of the 'Stephen Stills' album —which was, in addition, 'dedicated to James Marshall Hendrix'.)

The only black mark Jimi got in 1968, as far as the public was concerned, was (apart from the Anaheim no-visuals complaints back in February) that many fans in Britain grew increasingly to feel that Jimi had 'deserted' them. A lot of people in Britain wondered why Jimi and the Experience spent so much time in America. Many fans expressed their disenchantment in letters to the pop papers; and even some writers and music critics voiced their dismay at the long lapses between Jimi's infrequent British appearances.

This was, of course, a dissatisfaction that always occurs in Britain when groups, who first make it big in the UK, go away for long periods of time to make bigger fortunes and play larger auditoriums in the United States. And as for infrequent appearances, Jimi was not so 'guilty' as others. The fans of Bob Dylan, for instance, had to wait from 1966 until 1969 for a British appearance of their idol—and then that long-awaited return was for a one-hour performance at the Isle of Wight.

Jimi, on the other hand, *did* appear in Britain in 1968; the Experience were the featured act at a rock festival held at

Woburn Abbey. As had happened before, the fans gave Jimi and the group a tremendous reception but Jimi was less than delighted by their performance. When he spoke to me about it in New York, he said:

'We hadn't played together as a group for quite some time and we just couldn't seem to get into it. Now that I look back on it, well, maybe we were trying too hard, because at the time we did it, it was more like a jam than a concert.'

In any case, Jimi had an answer to those fans who complained at his not spending much time in Britain that year. He told the press:

'I am an American. And I would like for people there to see me. I also felt that although we had been accepted in Britain and Europe, we had not totally made it; and wanted to see if the people in America would really dig us.

'I dig Britain, but I haven't really got a home. I feel that the earth's my home. I don't want to really plant roots, because I know that I'm likely to get restless and want to move on. I'll only think about doing the house thing when I'm certain I want to settle down in a particular place. And,' he added, candidly, 'one of the main reasons we work in America is a very important reason—we can make much more money; and we are just like everyone else, we have to eat and pay our bills too. Plus, in America there are so many different places that you can play that you seldom have to play the same places the way you do in Britain.'

Meanwhile, away in America or not, the records kept selling, and kept coming, in Britain as well as everywhere else. The *Axis: Bold as Love* album had gone gold, the *Smash Hits* album had itself been a smash hit and, in October, a new single was released in Britain.

The A-side was the chilling Bob Dylan composition, *All along the Watchtower* and whereas Dylan's own version, issued earlier in the year on his *John Wesley Harding* album, got its effectiveness from its relentless pared-down quality and its understatement, Hendrix's version wedded Dylan's icy lyrics with his own brilliant and searing guitar-work. Hendrix had always admitted that Dylan had been a heavy influence on him, and he certainly did justice to this, one of Dylan's greatest songs, adding his own magic touch. Indeed many reviewers considered that Jimi's version was definitive —that he had made the song his own.

'Tremendously exciting guitar figures here,' trumpeted a typical review of the single, 'plus a typically direct Hendrix vocal. The Dylan song, already a hit for Hendrix in the States, is pretty well spot on for Jimi. Lovely bass runs plus some furious percussion work. In fact this long-awaited release is virtually already a smash ... Predicted to be a massive seller in Britain.'

The B-side of the record was a Hendrix composition, *Hot Summer Night*.

In fact it entered the British Top 50 way down at Number 48, on 26 October, but jumped from there to Number 18 in a week and was right up at Number 6 the week after.

The same day, 9 November, the *Electric Ladyland* double-album was released, and was immediately engulfed in controversy because of its cover. The cover photograph featured twenty or so nude girls, slightly distorted by some camera technique, and resulted in most record-shops refusing to display the album, even though their moral outrage was sufficiently quelled by the profit-motive to allow them to sell the record anyway. They just tucked it away like some dirty book.

When I asked Jimi what he thought of the cover design, he told me: 'I didn't like it much but there was nothing I could do. They never consulted me about those kind of things.'

The *Electric Ladyland* album itself revealed a lot about the changes Hendrix had been going through during the summer of '68. For one thing, it backed up the evidence provided by the *All along the Watchtower* single that Jimi was no longer only interested in his own material (a phase he had gone through earlier, after he had grown to hate *Hey Joe*). Apart from *Hey Joe* and the Noel Redding song *She's so Fine* all Hendrix's recordings with the Experience had been of his own compositions. But on this new double-album, there was not only another Redding song (in spite of all their mutual aggressiveness), called *Little Miss Strange*, but also the Dylan number *and* a song by Earl King, *Come on*.

Moreover, some of those musicians Hendrix had been jamming with did indeed turn up on the album, as had been predicted. In contrast to Jimi's feelings when the Experience had been formed, that more than three in the band would slow things down and get in the way, *Electric Ladyland* augmented the Experience with Mike Finnigan, Larry Faucette, Freddie Smith, Buddy Miles, Stevie Winwood, Jack Casady and Al Kooper.

Jimi's own comments on the album were to the effect that it was something he had always wanted to do. 'I felt that I didn't have to worry about limiting my arrangements so that we could get so many tracks on each side of the record. It was a new experience, a great sense of freedom.'

He also said, 'All of the tracks on the album are very personal to me, and I feel that this is really us. This album is very different from anything we've ever done before. It even starts off with a ninety-second sound-painting of the heavens.'

He paused. 'Now I know,' he went on, 'it's the kind of thing that people will want to jump on and start criticising right away, so I am going to say what I have to say before they start. I don't say it's great, but it is us.'

It was inevitable that there should have come a point at which Jimi wanted to produce his own records as well as compose, write, arrange and star on them—and by the time he had tasted the relative freedom that the *Electric Ladyland* album had offered him, it was obvious that he was more than ready to take over in the control booth.

Chas Chandler, who had produced the records up till then, had felt for some time that Jimi wanted to do the productions himself and, although Jimi never did come right out and say it, he made it known to Chandler in little subtle ways that he would be happier if Chas wasn't involved in the production of their records any more ...

It was, as Chandler had been the first to perceive, time for him to bow out. There had been all manner of disagreements and tensions; it had been a strain on Chandler, trying to guide someone as volatile and immoderate as Hendrix, and trying, too, to hold the increasingly warring factions of the Experience together. There had, as well, been mounting differences of policy and attitude between Chas Chandler and Mike Jeffries as to how the management should be. So now, being effectively shouldered out of the record-production side of things as well was, as they say, the last straw. Chandler sold his 50 per cent of Jimi's management contract to Mike Jeffries (who therefore now controlled the lot) and stepped out of the picture graciously. He was later to be involved in Noel Redding's own group, the ill-fated Fat Mattress, and then, eventually, groom and lead to stardom the currently idolised band Slade.

If dumping Chandler caused Jimi Hendrix any private regret (which almost certainly it did—it was even rumoured later in his career that he asked Chandler to come back, but that Chandler refused) it didn't hinder his public success.

The same month that the *Electric Ladyland* album was issued in Britain, Jimi finally did get the Keys to the City of Seattle—an amazing achievement for an alleged hoaxer and obscenity-seller. And being black was no asset. 'Has he acquired the art of fooling all the people all the time?' wrote one jaundiced reviewer—but no-one took any notice.

'I wonder if my old school-teacher digs me getting the Freedom of Seattle,' Jimi mused. 'She was a good-looker ...

Maybe she's a Daughter of the American Revolution now!'

A journalist, talking to Hendrix at the same time, told him for some reason that Petula Clark, the British singer, was a prospective member of any Hendrix Hate Society that might be going.

'Well I figure it's nice of her to have thought enough about me to say anything,' said Jimi. 'But I dig her. I think she's great and progressive—which is more than I can say about a lot of pop stars. Take Presley,' he went on. 'He's still got plenty of fans, but the only progress he's made is on his bank statement. That's not my scene. Nobody who is continually experimenting with music makes big money, but they get respect in the right quarters ... Britain, for instance. I was completely unknown in America until the word got around that the British dug my kind of music.'

At the same time as his Seattle award, Hendrix was voted the World's No. 1 Musician by the readers of the music paper *Disc* in Britain. And by the end of the year, they'd collected a whole lot more similar accolades. In the *Record Mirror* poll, the Experience was voted 7th Best Instrumental Group, Jimi was voted No. 2 in the Solo Instrumentalist category, No. 19 for Best Male Vocalist, and (an added bonus which really delighted him) No. 11 in the paper's Best-Dressed category. In the eyes of *Melody Maker*'s readers, meanwhile, Hendrix ended 1968 by being the 2nd Most Popular Musician in the World. Finally, when the editorial caucus of America's ultra-hip rock magazine *Rolling Stone* got around to making *their* awards for 1968, Hendrix was winner of their American and British Rock 'n' Roll Album of the Year category with the *Electric Ladyland* double-album, and, appearing on their cover to back it all up, was also declared their Performer of the Year.

'... We had not totally made it,' Jimi had said earlier in the year, 'and I wanted to see if the people in America would really dig us.' He had now got his answer. Everybody loved him by the end of 1968. He was a universal superstar. Awards from everywhere; votes galore; and—yes, you guessed it, *Electric Ladyland* was a Gold Record too—record sales unabated.

If this was just a fairy-tale, the present chapter would end right there. But in truth, the immense pile-up of difficulties which was to cascade down around Jimi's shoulders throughout 1969—which was, in contrast to '68, his least successful and least productive year—had already begun to activate itself. 1968 had provided, for Jimi, love aplenty; but there was much confusion also. By the closing months of the year, there were a number of crises, as well as lesser setbacks, that were beginning to take their toll on Jimi Hendrix.

Late in the year, Jimi was involved in a street accident. It wasn't a major one, but it put him, briefly, into hospital with torn leg ligaments. Around the same time, he was banned by Carnegie Hall and told that he would not be able to perform there in the future, regardless of how much he had erased the 'obscenity' from his stage-act.

On top of that, there was the resignation of Chandler from Jimi's affairs—which must have had the effect of removing one of Jimi's few anchors to stability. Chas had helped Hendrix in far more ways than merely financial ones. He had eased him into the British music scene with genuine consideration and understanding in the first instance; he had taken a sympathetic interest in the creative side of Jimi's affairs; in so doing, as I noted earlier in this book, he served as an invaluable counterbalance to the purely monetary manoeuvring of Mike Jeffries; and he had maintained, throughout the period from late '66 until late '68, both a strong faith in, and friendship for, Jimi the musician and Jimi the private individual underneath. And there's no doubt that Jimi felt the loss of all those qualities when, finally, Chandler was exhausted and eased out.

In addition, the deteriorating relationship between Jimi and Noel Redding had unquestionably reached crisis point. Noel had had enough of being instructed by Jimi as to exactly what notes to play when—had had enough of this creative subservience and of taking a background role. He wanted to go back to playing lead guitar instead of bass, and he wanted to do it fronting his own group, Fat Mattress.

Mitch Mitchell, too, had grown more and more restless, even though he had always enjoyed more freedom than Noel within the Experience—he had, after all, been hired in the first place because Hendrix liked his 'free-form style of playing'. All the same, by late 1968, Mitch was keen to form *his* own group, and also to get into doing some producing.

Another factor which was beginning to impinge heavily on the group by the end of 1968 was the black power movement in the United States. There had been numerous riots and bloody confrontations between blacks and whites in many major cities. Both Noel and Mitch felt that things were getting very heavy there, and they both saw the black power movement as designed to pit the hippies (who were 98 per cent white youths) against the black people of the same generation, and they were not into having any of that scene. It had only been a short while before that Jimi had been able to say that: 'The flower scene was an experiment but although it was all tied up with sensation stuff about drugs, the love everybody basic idea helped one hell of a lot with the colour problem in the States. Coloured artists didn't dare go near some Southern audiences in the past, but since the flower power craze much of the violence has gone.'

Yet now it was, seemingly, back again, on a more political plane. And it was becoming more and more embarrassing for the Experience to do concerts. For Mitch and Noel it was becoming something they felt pressured into feeling self-conscious about—two white boys, two rich white boys, backing up a black superstar. For Jimi himself it was becoming equally difficult. The militant younger generation of black Americans were starting to make demands on him: they expected him to care more about his blackness than about his music; they resented his not using black musicians; and they disliked the fact that he had always appealed far more to middle-class whites—the hippies—than to his 'true brothers'.

It was this snowballing pressure which was finally to split the Experience and which was also to create a lot of trouble and pain for Jimi himself as 1969 wore on.

As early as November of '68 it was strongly rumoured that the Experience was to disband except for a few selected gigs. In February 1969, the split was finally announced, along with the news that they would play two farewell concerts at the Royal Albert Hall in London, followed by a farewell tour of the States.

At the time of the split it was generally reported inside music business circles that although Jimi had been making the lion's share of the bread, Noel Redding was actually much better off than either of the others, because, remembering the bad old days vividly, he had been relentlessly thrifty. Jimi himself, on the other hand, had lately been spending money more extravagantly than ever. Mitch, just as he had taken a middle course in other ways—in having more opportunity for creative expression in the group than Noel yet less than Jimi; in keeping quiet when the other two were having their flare-up rows—had taken a middle course financially too. He hadn't pinched and saved assiduously like Noel; nor had he thrown his money away with anything approaching the abandon that Jimi had managed.

He was, however, as keen as either of the others, to pursue his own music. Talking to the press about his plans at this time, he said:

'Getting a group together is an outlet for me ... There are

lots of guitarists: maybe not as good as Jimi, but I can get up and play with them, and play differently all the time. Because one thing satisfies you, and you're happy, it doesn't mean others can't produce the same effect. It's rather like women.'

The musicians Mitch considered for his group were Eddie Thornton (trumpet), Derek Wadsworth (trombone) and Graham Bond (organ), plus, of course, a guitarist and a bass-player. Mitch had played with both Eddie and Derek during the early days when he was with Georgie Fame's Blue Flames, and at a certain house in Kensington they could be heard jumping and shaking till the wee hours of the morning.

'Lots of people were doing that sort of thing,' said Mitch. 'Georgie Fame and Alan Price had a floating band—it's a good thing. Nobody's gonna find out what they want to do if they just sit around on their arse all day.'

When it came to the farewell concert of the Experience at the Albert Hall, Mitch's parents and uncle attended—and so did many stars. As in the early days, many top musicians came to see Hendrix and the Experience do their thing—including Cat Stevens (who had, of course, been on the same bill as the group when they had done their *first* British concerts), Chris Wood, Denny Laine and Dave Mason.

Jimi explained to me some weeks afterwards why he had agreed to do these last Albert Hall gigs.

'They said it would be a good idea,' he told me, 'because I hadn't appeared in Britain for a while, and it would help my record sales. Well, I figured it wouldn't hurt to have the bread—and it would be kinda nice to see old England again.'

And not for the bread, but in an entirely unofficial capacity, Chas Chandler was there too for the final show, just to see that things went down properly. It was from this brief reunion that the rumours started that Jimi had asked Chandler to come back as his manager but that Chandler had refused.

Even if the rumours were not in fact true, there were grounds for thinking them likely to be. For one thing, Jimi had never been very happy with Mike Jeffries' methods of handling him. For another—and this was more fundamentally important—Jimi had increasingly reacted to the unhappiness of being a superstar on whom everybody made demands by trying to get back to old friends. He had, as noted earlier in this book, returned in the summer of 1967 to Ed Chalpin's studios and recorded again with me; he had derived an immense amount of spiritual comfort from his return to his family and his home-town of Seattle the following year; and after the break-up of the Experience, when he did get together an all-black band, the bass-player he turned to was his old friend from his paratrooper days in the US Army, Billy Cox. And it wasn't long after that before he brought Mitch Mitchell back into the fold, playing mostly, in the last twelve months of his career, with Cox and Mitchell together.

But those developments are documented later. Back, now, to the Albert Hall ...

Jimi's opening numbers were harsh and brutal, but then things began to mellow out, and slanted into some very hip blues. The set lasted well over an hour, and with the audience shouting out requests, Jimi had to play what had become standards at any Hendrix concert—*Foxy Lady*, *Purple Haze*, *Fire*, *Hey Joe* and the rest.

The audience responded as wildly as you would expect. One fan got so carried away that he was dancing high up over the stage and, when he was forcibly removed by an attendant, the crowd booed loudly. It was a great concert.

It was also, as Valerie Mabbs reported to readers of *Record Mirror* on 15 March 1969, a very busy and hectic day for Hendrix on the Monday of that final concert.

'Jimi,' she reported, 'was involved in a recording and film

session. "The concert at the Albert Hall was taped for probably our next LP," explained Jimi. "We'll also be working on some studio sessions, but I already have a number in mind for our next single. I'd like to break up *Stone Free* and put it out like an American single." '

Jimi went on to explain to *Record Mirror* his disappointment at the way that the British pressing of the *Electric Ladyland* double album turned out.

' "We wanted to handle the editing and mixing ourselves but unfortunately we were unable to spend the time on it. The engineers retaped the whole original tape before they pressed the record for Britain, and so much sound was lost. Now I'm learning more about this kind of thing so that I can handle it myself." At the same time as the concert recording was made, Jimi was filmed in action. This won't be his only venture in films, though as Jimi explained: "I'm going to be featured in a western-type movie soon. The Experience hope to write the soundtrack for the film, but we won't be depicted as musicians—that's Mickie Mouse stuff. I'll probably play a half-breed bandit." '

Jimi talked a whole lot more in that same interview— about his music, his future, technology and thought-control, and his desire to have a short rest in Britain before going back to the States:

'I really feel unlimited. British audiences tend to think they know and have heard everything. If they'd listen properly, though, I'm sure they'd learn much more. We've always tried to be honest through our music, and if people don't understand, it shows they haven't been listening. The music in itself has a lot to say, even if it has a seven-word repetitive lyric ...

'I've been through a lot of changes. The things I've

learned, I've tried to convey to the people in my own way. It's my own solution until something else comes along ...

'There must be so much more' (about life in general—the future) 'that people don't understand yet. At the moment people use only a minute part of their mind and there's so much more scope. If only people wouldn't concentrate on the superficial things, they might find the real meaning and true happiness. Things like witchcraft, which is a form of exploration, and imagination, have been banned by the establishment and called evil. It's because people are frightened to find out the full power of the mind ...

'Somebody told me when I was in America that scientists have apparently found a way to harness some thought-impulses. They got people to switch channels on a television set. In fact the buttons were dead, but a certain impulse created by the thought process worked the set. There are so many possibilities to be derived from this kind of thing ...'

Kathy Etchingham was with Jimi the night of that last Albert Hall concert, and on the way home together after the show they had a strange and comic encounter. As they were turning into the street where they were staying, walking quietly in the dead of night, with Kathy carrying the roses that had been sent backstage by a fan, and Jimi carrying his guitar, they were stopped by the police. Apparently Richard Milhous Nixon, that other American with a somewhat different kind of notoriety from Jimi's, was in London and, as Jimi explained to me with amusement, 'they were taking very strict security measures to ensure the great white father's safety. The police recognised me and started laughing. They asked was I carrying a machine-gun in my guitar-case? I said "Yeah, I'm John Dillinger". Anyway they searched me before they let us go.'

Jimi stayed in London for a short while after that, just grooving around and giving the occasional interview; but mostly his mind was on his Electric Ladyland studios then under construction in Greenwich Village in New York. So it was to New York that he then returned.

It was during his short and spasmodic string of concert appearances on the American side of the Atlantic that he flew into Toronto, Canada, and was busted at the airport for possession of heroin and hash.

CHAPTER SEVEN

The Mounties almost get their man

The Canadian police are renowned the world over for always getting their man. Well, this is the story of one who got away—Jimi Hendrix.

Jimi told me afterwards that he had really been looking forward to going to Toronto, because he knew that he had many, many fans there, and he also had a number of friends in the city. But, he said, if he'd known that he was going to have all the problems that he did have as a result of that trip, he would certainly never have gone.

It all started when they got off the plane—they had flown in from Los Angeles—at Toronto International Airport. Now Jimi had got used to being hassled by customs officials in various countries; and in fact the United States customs men had taken him through more hassles more often than any other officials in any other countries. But this Canadian encounter was something new.

According to Jimi, this is what happened. As he got off the plane with his entourage, he was only carrying his flight bag, but he figured that they might well stop him anyway, because they usually stopped all long-haired freaks and definitely anyone they thought was a musician. (Needless to say, the guys who really bring the big stuff in look nothing whatever like a customs man's stereotyped image of the long-haired druggy freak.)

Jimi said: 'When the guy started going through my flight bag, the only thing that I was thinking about was "I wish he would hurry up"—so that I could just get to the hotel and crash; because I had taken some Mandrax a few hours earlier and I wanted to get a few hours sleep before the concert that night.'

Mandrax, of course, is now very hard to obtain as a sleeping tablet, because it has been massively used as a way to get high—rather a drunken kind of high, that is: nothing like the calming spiritual effects achieved by the more 'illegal' drugs.

'Anyway,' Jimi told me, 'suddenly this cat said "Well now! What is this?!", and he pulled out of my flight bag a bottle that I didn't even know was there. So he took me into the main customs office and this straight Establishment-looking dude said, after a few preliminary questions: "Well I'm sorry Mr Hendrix, we will have to detain you until we can analyse the substances in this bottle and in these packets." So there I was in the clutches of the pigs.

'Well,' Jimi continued, 'it didn't take them long to find out that it was hashish and heroin, and they officially arrested me and said I would have to stand trial later. Well my manager managed to get me out of jail by putting up a lot of bread,'—Hendrix was released on bail of 10,000 dollars —'which guaranteed that I would show up for the trial.'

Jimi didn't have time to get the sleep he had counted on at the hotel, and though he made it in time to the concert that night—it was held at the Maple Leaf Gardens, Toronto—he was pretty near exhausted.

Not surprisingly, Jimi said: 'I did the concert anyway but I couldn't really get into it.'

There was another reason besides his tiredness for his not

getting into his music that night : an equally understandable reason.

'It was hard,' Jimi explained, 'because I was thinking what if they decided to make an example of me? Because the minute I was arrested, it was all over the radios, newspapers and television. I didn't even think they would let me do the concert, but it was a sell-out and Canada would have lost a lot of tax bread, so I guess that's why they let me do it.

'Anyway I was happy to get out of Canada—because I had heard of heavy police scenes in Canada where they lock the door and throw the key away.'

There were a million different rumours flying around after this Jimi Hendrix Canadian Dope Encounter Part One. (Part Two, of course, was the trial, later.)

One of the most persistent was that, unlike in the United States, where money and sharp lawyers could probably have got Hendrix out of anything, there was in Canada none of that sort of corruption—and nobody to write the kind of sympathetic and influential editorial that Mick Jagger received from *The Times*—so that if Jimi was found guilty, that would really be it. He'd have to languish in jail, perhaps for a very long time.

Another rumour, apparently not true, as it turned out, was that Jimi went off to a secret studio to record a large but undisclosed number of new songs, so that in case Jimi did have to go to jail for the minimum sentence of seven years (the usual penalty handed out in cases of that nature, involving heroin), the record company would have enough recorded material on hand to release for years to come. Because neither they nor Jimi himself wanted to lose the lucrative earnings they would miss out on if there was a seven-year silence from Hendrix. You can't spin out compilation albums that long, however hard you might be prepared to try.

Hendrix, in any event, took his departure from Canada, and what happened between that point—early May 1969—

and his re-appearance for his trial in Toronto at the end of the year, is told in the next chapter. We jump ahead now to the trial itself : the Jimi Hendrix Canadian Dope Encounter Part Two.

The case was scheduled to be heard on 8 December 1969, in Toronto, and as well as Jimi himself, witnesses were flown in from the United States and England for the trial. It was a spectacular occasion—as were most controversial occasions where Jimi was involved—and the courtroom was surrounded by the love children of the flower era, who showed up to give moral support to Jimi. As he arrived they cheered and waved, flashing the sign of peace. They wanted their hero and brother to know that his trip was their trip. And Jimi smiled and waved back and knew that he was not alone.

His supporters tried to pack into the public gallery of the court, but there were far too many people chasing far too little space, so that the great majority were disappointed. However, without any undue rioting, the trial eventually got under way.

Jimi's defence, characteristically of him, was simply to tell the truth. He didn't pretend that he had never touched drugs in his life; nor did he try to claim that the whole thing was a political trial in which his only 'crime' was being black.

When he was asked if he had ever taken drugs, Jimi admitted immediately to having taken marijuana, hashish, LSD and cocaine, but said—as he had always said in private —that he was not into heroin at all.

He also told the court, perhaps more from a vantage-point of wishful thinking than of literal truth, that he had now outgrown drugs altogether and was on a strictly mental high: a perpetual spiritual high.

He went on to testify that on many occasions, he and other members of the group had received many gifts of drugs from fans—cakes and cookies that were made from hashish or grass, and presents in many different forms that contained LSD or other highs.

That, he said, was the only way he could account for what the customs men had discovered in his flight bag back at the airport in May. Jimi testified that he had done a concert in Los Angeles on 1 May and that after the concert:

'I had a real bad stomach and this chick that was in my hotel room at the time gave me this bottle and told me to take it because it would make me feel better. I thought it was Bromoseltzer or something and dropped it in my flight bag without even opening it—and I just forgot all about it, until that customs guy pulled it out of my bag that day when I was going through customs.'

Jimi's account was corroborated, fortunately enough, by a woman reporter from Los Angeles who testified that she was also in Hendrix's hotel room at the time and had seen him being given this bottle with a yellow cap on it—the bottle in question.

On 11 December 1969, Jimi Hendrix was acquitted, and the last glimpse that the officials and the fans there had of him was as he left the court with two of his inevitable foxy ladies, flashing the V for Victory sign.

And that indeed was the right ending to a case where the Mounties almost got their man. As the rhyme goes,

> Catch a fox
> Put him in a box
> And then we'll let him go.

CHAPTER EIGHT

The burning of the midnight lamp

Before the Toronto bust, Jimi Hendrix had taken over a new house in Brook Street in London. Or rather, a very old house. As the *Daily Mirror* put it in their headline which accompanied an interview with Jimi at the time: 'Hallelujah! It's Hendrix in Handel's old house!'

(Jimi was in good form for the interview. 'To tell you the God's honest truth, I haven't heard much of the fella's stuff,' he told the reporter. 'I didn't even know this was his pad, man, until after I got in.')

He stayed there—this was back in January 1969—with Kathy Etchingham (and had introduced her to the *Daily Mirror* reporter as being: 'My girl-friend, my past girl-friend, and probably my next girl-friend, my mother and sister and all that bit. My Yoko Ono from Chester.'). But the house in Brook Street was more an extravagance than a place he really intended to live in, and after the concert in Toronto in May, Jimi based himself firmly in New York. He kept his breathtakingly hip, futuristic pad in the city, but retired quietly to a house in Liberty, upstate. Noel and Mitch returned to Britain to pursue their own separate plans.

Jimi didn't seem to have any plans. Pete Townshend told

me: 'I saw him once or twice, wandering about, like, in New York. You'd go down into the Village and there he'd be, wandering about, getting as much life as he could possibly get into the few years that he did have.'

He would visit the city from time to time, staying briefly in his classy apartment there, but mostly he stayed in Liberty, just resting and trying to get his head together again.

He was also trying to work out his next move—which by this point meant working out where he stood as regards the black movement.

Jimi had been criticised for supposedly turning his back on his black brothers—and it bothered him increasingly: because he didn't seem to fit into any of the slots. Although it was very hard to get Jimi into a conversation on this subject, I know from being around him that the whole thing bothered him a lot. On the one hand, it worried him that Jimi's American fans were about 90 per cent white and therefore at most 10 per cent black. And various black organisations in the USA had made it clear by this point in time that they considered Jimi to be in a uniquely powerful position on the music scene—and that they felt that Jimi, as a brother, could do the black cause a lot of good if he was publicly affiliated with them and participated, both financially and musically, in the movement.

But this worried Hendrix too because, although Jimi was proud of being black, he was definitely not into a colour-conscious trip.

Nevertheless, what Jimi decided, after wrestling with all these pressures, was that he ought to try to do an all-black thing—musically. That was about as far as he wanted to go. It was rumoured that he was involved with the Black Panther Party, but though I couldn't absolutely disprove those rumours, I feel pretty convinced that they simply weren't true. Jimi's whole way of thinking, his spiritual philosophy, his love for people as people, his dislike of being on a colour-conscious trip, and his avoidance of any kind of *organisation*, all testify to the improbability of his getting into any kind of solid rapport with the Panthers. He just couldn't be that committed. It is significant, in fact, that even when Jimi had decided to get an all-black group to-gether behind him, he rarely performed with them (as we shall see later on in this chapter). Far more often, in this last eighteen months of his life, he played with Mitch Mitchell on drums (because to Jimi the sound was far more important than the cat's colour) and with Billy Cox on bass—and though Billy is black, he was brought in by Jimi for the much stronger reason that he was an old friend and as such was a kind of anchor that Jimi could hold onto.

Indeed, if we look ahead for a moment to May 1970, we find that it was actually announced (though it didn't come off) that the original Experience would re-form.

So for those many reasons, it doesn't seem at all realistic to think that Jimi involved himself in any meaningful way with the Black Panther Party. And what he did do—which shows his rather different line of thinking—was send a cheque for 5,000 dollars to the Martin Luther King Foundation: because Martin Luther King was a man for whom Jimi had had the greatest admiration and respect.

Jimi started playing with Mitch Mitchell again around June 1969, and it was at that point that he brought in Billy Cox. The all-black thing was to be another six months away.

Billy Cox had been Jimi's friend and fellow-paratrooper way back in their military service days. When I talked to him about his first-ever meeting with Jimi, Billy said:

'We were both stationed at Fort Campbell, Kentucky, and I was walking by one of the service clubs one day and I heard someone playing some incredible guitar inside. So when I went in to check it out, it turned out to be Jimi. I introduced myself to him and told him that I was a bass player; so then I checked a bass out from the service club—

they had almost every instrument that you could imagine for any of the servicemen that wished to use them. We had a really nice jam, and after we finished, we decided to put a group together from servicemen stationed with us. We found an officer that played sax, and a drummer, and after a few rehearsals, we started playing at the service clubs and different places. We got to be pretty good.'

What Jimi said about his early meeting with Billy Cox was:

'I liked Billy's solid style of playing bass. He could really keep a nice groove going. Even though he wasn't what you call a spectacular bass player, he kept things nicely together.'

When you compare how closely Jimi's assessment of Billy's playing parallels his assessment of Noel Redding's when the auditions for The Experience were first held, it makes sense that Jimi should bring back Billy Cox after the demise of The Experience. And it makes more sense because, as we've noted, by this point in time, Jimi wanted to have musicians around him that he knew and felt he could get along with on a personal basis.

In July, this new line-up played the Newport '69 Festival, and in August they played Woodstock. Between times, Jimi spent some time in California and some back in upstate New York, surrounded, at this point, by 'the electric family'—a houseful of musicians and writers: friends, old blues guys, hangers-on, modern classical composers, freaks and African musicians.

At the same time, Jimi was getting together his long-dreamed-of Electric Ladyland Studios in New York City, producing the Eire Apparent album *Sunrise* and managing a band called Cat Mother—though it's hard to imagine Jimi in the role of manager/businessman, in any normal sense of the word.

Despite all this activity, 1969 was Jimi's least productive year since fame had first borne him on her magic wings. But

Woodstock was a beautiful exception to that unproductive, untogether situation. Woodstock was a golden interlude between the hassles and the doubts—and wings of magic certainly touched Jimi's being once again.

Woodstock, the most famous of all the rock festivals, held not far from Jimi's house in Liberty, on a site of farmland with rolling hills and fringed by a lake and trees: the perfect combination of amenities for a very special weekend.

Natural amenities, however, were not, of course, enough. An incredible amount of organisation, planned and supervised by the energetic young promoters of the festival, swung into action on a vast scale. The laying-on and synchronisation of electrical power was handled by the largest group of electricians and technicians ever assembled for an outdoor event, with many of them working on a voluntary basis. Stewards, stage-crew, fence-erectors—just an incredible number of people at work, to do all the necessary preparations for accommodating the vast influx expected of young people from all over the nation—urban flower children escaping from the steaming side-walks, the congestion and the cockroaches of New York City; commune-livers from far-flung outposts of the huge Mid-West; and even persevering sojourners all the way from San Francisco.

And 400,000 people came.

400,000 film-stars in one epic: that was what the film of the festival, simply called *Woodstock*, showed. It showed the whole historic occasion on film, and showed that the air of togetherness and the good vibe that epitomised that magical weekend came not just from the many star performers and groups who appeared (flown in by a ferry-service of helicopters organised and timed as precisely and finely as a large-scale military operation) but from the audience itself. Woodstock was like a city of peace, and one can just feel the greatness and importance of the event by watching the film. Not surprisingly, that film has been enjoyed by more world-wide rock music lovers than any other in the history of pop's documentation on celluloid.

Jimi Hendrix had always loved festivals—had believed in them, and in their special capacity for letting his music communicate to his audience—and at this best and most momentous of all the festivals, Jimi was the undoubted star and the undoubted spiritual leader. Even measured in mere financial terms, Jimi was the highlight of the weekend—the highest-paid performer, receiving 18,000 dollars. And in musical terms, Jimi provided the highlight of the festival too, with his unbelievable rendition of *The Star-Spangled Banner*, which was both a dazzling display of pyrotechnics and also, inseparably, a brilliantly original and moving expression of his generation's agonised feelings for their country—for the gulf between the flower children's aspirations and the realities of what was going down in Nixon's America.

Woodstock said it all, and in Jimi's music, *he* said it all for Woodstock.

In very sharp contrast, there had been, earlier in the year, another festival in another place—the city of Denver, Colorado—when Jimi had been forced to 'say it all' in a very different way.

The Denver 'Festival', in early June '69, had been one of the last concerts that The Experience had played in America during their farewell programme of sporadic gigs, and the vibe was very different from Woodstock.

Denver is a place I know well, because when my father split from my mother when I was four years old, he moved there and has been there ever since, now running a little jive-ass drive-in barbecue joint in the Five Points (the heart of the black section). Denver is way out in the Mid-West, no other cities for many, many miles, a tourist attraction, its elevation more than a mile high, and surrounded by beautiful snow-capped mountains, with pollution-free air and fresh spring water.

A nice place, that is to say, for a festival—except that the Mid-West police are something else, and at the time Jimi Hendrix played there, none of the Denver authorities were used to dealing with any kind of influx of young people. In fact, the Denver police didn't know their ass from a hole in the ground so far as security at a rock concert was concerned. They treated the situation like it was a major invasion from Mars.

When Jimi talked to me about the gig, this was his account of what happened:

'Man, I really liked that clear fresh air in Denver, and things were going so beautiful that I never anticipated such an ending to a concert.

'We were playing, and there must have been forty or fifty thousand people there, and man, those damn police had a line of cops around the stage like they were SS troops in World War II. And they were really hassling the kids.

'They wouldn't even let them breathe! Suddenly, a few kids were really grooving, and tried to get a little closer to the stage. Instead of letting us handle it, the police suddenly started shooting tear-gas in the crowd, like it was a fucking real war. Naturally everyone started running in a panic to get away from that tear-gas, and it was coming back at us because the wind was blowing in our direction. And we all freaked, because the people were running towards the stage trying to get away.

'Imagine that many people running and mad at the damn police and wanting to destroy anything and anybody in their path, to get back at the police for fucking up their concert!

'So we all jumped in the equipment van and they locked us in—and I don't know yet how we were able to get out of there without really getting hurt, because they had to drive us through the crowd, who almost smashed the van to pieces.'

So Jimi wasn't able to 'say it all' with his music that time in Denver, because they interrupted his music and broke up the concert. Jimi had to say it another way—and the behaviour of the police had made pretty clear to Jimi how much it needed saying. What he did was, in his own words:

'I later sent a telegram to the Denver Chief of Police that said: "Make Love Not War. Peace—Jimi Hendrix".'

In December of that year, 1969, after Jimi's acquittal from that *other* brush with the police, back in Toronto, he was back in New York again, and at last got together his all-black thing. He organised a group he called the Band of Gypsies. The group consisted of Jimi on lead guitar and vocals, Buddy Miles on drums and vocals, and Billy Cox again on bass.

Jimi and Buddy Miles had first met in New York, and had known each other for a while by this point. Miles was then, and still is, a Mercury Recording artist, and had cut several albums with varying degrees of success prior to joining Jimi and the Band of Gypsies, and had been a prominent member of the famous Electric Flag band. He had also scored a notable success with a single of his own song *Them Changes*, which had made the US charts.

He brought with him to the Jimi Hendrix Band of Gypsies a very dynamic, black, evangelistic southern soulful camp-meeting style of singing—when you heard Buddy Miles sing, you thought you were at a southern Baptist religious camp-meeting and revival, where they play slide trombones and beat tambourines and tremendous emotion and religious fervour is exhibited. He also brought to the Band of Gypsies a style of drumming that was his own and which had already gained him the respect of fellow-musicians. He was what I call a non-flash drummer, a drummer who kept more or less to a deceptively simple basic beat. And he was also a very colourful performer.

Some people were to say that Buddy Miles' style of drum-

ming was never truly compatible with Jimi's guitar-style.
Perhaps they were right: certainly the Band of Gypsies
didn't last long, and was to break up in disarray in the
middle of a concert, as we shall see. Yet to attribute this
brevity of the group's life, and its failure to ever really make
it, musically, solely to Buddy's incompatibility as regards
Jimi's style, is very much an unjust oversimplification.

It has to be remembered that Jimi was going through
changes and problems himself, in any case, and the Band of
Gypsies was more of an *attempt* to solve some of those
problems than a real solution. It was Jimi's attempt to do an
all-black thing—and as I said earlier, Jimi fundamentally
felt torn between his own personal musical desires and the
black pressures that were being exerted upon him by various
organisations and individuals.

It was a complex set of feelings that Jimi had to wrestle
with. It was true, for instance, that one of his favourite
groups was a group called The Last Poets, who came from the
ghettos of Harlem with a poetic musical message that used
street language in brilliant soul-searching songs, sung and
often chanted, in impressive unison, to the simple accom-
paniment of sometimes just one bongo drum. Their bag was
black awareness; their albums, though banned on 99 per
cent of the radio-stations in America, became best-sellers;
and they were much in demand at concerts and on the
college circuit. They were revolutionary—unique. Four
young men raised in the horrible filth and squalor of Harlem,
where drugs were more easily obtained than food and shelter
and other basic necessities of life.

What they did was, they gave black people shocking
examples of their over-indulgences in the more sensual
pleasures of life, while showing that at the same time they
allowed black education and economic growth, black power
and racial unity to go unstrived-for. The Last Poets urged
that instead of black people maintaining a 'fuck everybody

else; I'm gonna get what I can for myself' attitude, they should get themselves together and organised. They tried to get the black man to get his head out of his ass and his hand off his or someone else's sexual organs, and into getting it together for black people as a whole.

And despite Jimi Hendrix's dislike of what he regarded as 'colour-conscious trips', he really dug The Last Poets.

Part of why Jimi could identify with The Last Poets was because, like them, he felt Harlem-orientated. He had knocked around Harlem, he had felt the hard times of being poor and being black in New York City; and—a pleasant memory—Harlem was where Jimi had met Fayne, the slender and sexy black chick who had been Jimi's regular girl when I first met him.

Fayne had meant a lot to Jimi. Not only had she given him many hours of sensual delight, but she had also been the one who had got his hair together for him with her hot-comb and curlers, and had cooked him that soul food that he so often longed for.

Fayne's mother had found Jimi a bit strange, and had hoped that her daughter's involvement wouldn't last— but Jimi continued to see Fayne whenever he was in New York City. The first time he returned to the city from England, he went to see her and told her he'd brought her a present. It turned out to be some LSD, which was hardly what she'd expected; but Jimi was full of surprises, and always had been. He also introduced Kathy Etchingham to Fayne while Kathy was in New York, and the two became good friends.

Jimi was also still seeing Devon, 'the supergroupie', periodically. Devon was sort of commuting back and forth from New York to England and back, as the mood struck her —usually depending on where Jimi was. And by this time, Jimi had also met Monika (Jimi's German girl who would be the last person to see Hendrix alive), and though they had not had the opportunity to spend much time together, they had already developed a deep feeling for each other.

In the early days when Jimi was first in Britain, he told me that he usually told Kathy about most of his scenes with other chicks, because she understood that it was just his way and that he had to feel that he was free. But in time, despite the friendships of various chicks, and despite Jimi's insistence on being free and untangled in his relationships, it did all get a bit heavy.

Just how heavy can be gleaned from the vivid picture given by Pat Hartley—a twenty-seven-year-old New Yorker who, in her own words, 'wasn't a terribly successful groupie', but who was a friend of Devon's, and who knew Jimi quite well. Pat Hartley talked to Marion Fudger in *Spare Rib* magazine (August 1973) about Jimi, Devon, herself and the groupie chaos that surrounded them all :

'Jimi was too much for me to handle,' Pat said, 'and I knew it and I wasn't about to take the plunge. Talk to him or be friends with him, OK, but to get more involved than that ... Sometimes just talking to him was so heavy and strange, but I mean, he was an exceptional person. As well as being an exceptional guitarist, he was also incredibly funny, as good as any stand up comic I ever heard; but to get really involved, to be his girl-friend ... Well, Devon was his girl-friend and I tagged along behind Devon, so we just made it that way round ... I mean he called me up one night and said what are you doing in New York while your old man is in London, and I said sitting on the couch talking to you. Obviously, one would get obsessed with loyalty in that situation. Especially with so many chicks around ...

'There's about four or five sort of famous groupies and Devon was one of them, but she never lasted long with any-body. She didn't want to live with anybody, it was just a real status thing ...

'Jimi does a sort of thing in the documentary'—the film

'biography' issued in 1973, with accompanying soundtrack album—'which is a bit tongue in cheek humour, about how the door would open and there'd be this luscious girl standing there; "how could I resist it?" There's a facetious intelligence working there, it's well, lady you're all flinging yourself on my doorstep, how dare you then turn around and say to me that I'm in all kinds of trouble.

'Jimi was terribly obsessed with music, I mean he had something, the rest of us have nothing. Seems odd that people say he was an introvert. I wouldn't have the balls to say what I thought he was supposed to be ... The one thing I can tell you which I know is a fact is that he was in love with his music, that was all he wanted to do. He'd stay at the Scene until six in the morning, jamming with anybody, a piano stool, nothing. He thought about his music all day, hung round the clubs and then, oh, gotta go now and he'd rush down to the studio, play, play, play, until eleven in the morning and then go home to bed. He was really only interested in his music. He liked the idea of what was going on around him; what guy doesn't like the idea of fifty thousand chicks throwing themselves at you because you are Jimi Hendrix.

'He was shy, but that doesn't mean he wasn't going to beat you up if you took too much of a liberty with him. Michael Jeffries allowed very little about Jimi to come out— he was very isolated.'

At this point in the interview, Marion Fudger asked Pat what she meant by that, and Pat replied:

'It's so messy, it's got to do with Devon and six other chicks who Devon was pimping for Jimi and all kinds of weird shit going on and telephones ringing and girls being kicked downstairs and all kinds of nonsense. That's what it had to do with, and very late night acid trips and things like that ...

'Jimi knew perfectly well that if he told Collette to come

over on Thursday night at eight o'clock, Collette would call
Stella and Stella would tell Devon and Devon would come
over there and beat the door down and drag Jimi out to a
party. It was fun and some of it was an absolute horror ...
I dunno, it takes a lot of energy out of you.

'He wanted to do the same things we all wanted to do in
the same period of time but making music was what he
really wanted to do.

'Basically, he was looking for some kind of honesty from
anybody ... don't say something because you think you
should. It's embarrassing how few people were honest with
him at that time.

'Fayne was his first girl-friend. He wanted Devon and
Fayne to get together before he died because he thought
Fayne could put Devon back on the rails, 'cause she was
rapidly slipping off. She was totally involved with Jimi but
we didn't think about it like that, and then when he suddenly
died we realised that was what it was all about ... What's
going to happen, baby, if he doesn't get up one day at 11
o'clock. And that's what happened and everybody went
berserk ... it was all being held together by a piece of tissue
paper, namely Jimi's vibes.'

So certainly by the end of 1969, with less than a year to go
before Jimi died, and when he was launching the Band of
Gypsies, it did seem somewhat as if there was what you
could call a feminine web entangling Jimi's life in addition to
his other problems.

The début of the Band of Gypsies was at Bill Graham's
Fillmore East Theatre, located on 2nd Avenue and 6th Street,
in the East Village in New York City, on New Year's Eve:
31 December 1969. I can remember just how cold a night it
was.

Sharing the bill with Jimi's Band of Gypsies was an
incredible black group (from Harlem), called The Voices of
East Harlem—a group whose ages ranged from ten to nine-

teen, who wore blue jeans and all carried tambourines, and who, uniquely, entered the stage from the lobby, running down the aisles simultaneously with an incredible youthful zeal, creating a black church camp meeting atmosphere which the audience loved. Indeed, there was even a festive atmosphere among the huge crowd that waited outside in the freezing street hoping to get in by some miracle. And along with the masses of Jimi Hendrix fans, there were many famous names from the rock world present that night, glad to be able to see Jimi perform again and curious to find out what the Band of Gypsies was into.

The live album cut that night—which, when it was released in May 1970 was the first album Jimi's fans had had since the *Electric Ladyland* double-LP way back in the autumn of 1968—was issued not on Jimi's usual label, Warner Reprise, but on Capitol: the label that had always handled the releases from Ed Chalpin's studios.

This came about as a result of the in-court settlement between Mike Jeffries and Warner/Reprise Records and Ed Chalpin and Capitol Records, which had arisen because Jimi was under legal contract to Chalpin (as I was and still am) when he split to Britain with Chas Chandler in late 1966.

The conditions of the court settlement were as follows: Warner/Reprise were allowed to keep Jimi Hendrix as a recording artist but Capitol Records were to be given the next album (the *Band of Gypsies* live album); Mike Jeffries was to maintain management of Jimi but Ed Chalpin was to receive a payment of one million dollars, plus a percentage of Hendrix past, present and future. In addition, of course, the court upheld the right of Ed Chalpin to continue to issue those recordings in his possession which featured Jimi and me together.

That only settled the situation in America—and when, for instance, the 'Band of Gypsies' album was released in Britain, it was issued on Track Records just as the previous albums of the Jimi Hendrix Experience had been. For Europe and Britain, the case remained unsettled : it was pending, waiting to be heard as soon as it could be scheduled in the British courts. Again, I was to be a key witness in that case, having been the one who had found Jimi Hendrix and introduced him to Ed Chalpin back then in 1965—but, by a truly incredible stroke of fate, Mike Jeffries died in France in a mid-air collision the day before he was to give evidence in the court proceedings which were in progress at the time of his death in London.

But that is another digression; what all that explanation of the settlements was sparked off by was the début gig of the Band of Gypsies at the Fillmore East, back on New Year's Eve/New Year, 31 December '69/1 January 1970.

There was something about the magic of that performance —it was as if they somehow knew that they had got to get the best out of a group that was destined to have a very short musical life. As I stood backstage watching the concert, I was especially struck by the group's performance of the song *Machine Gun*. The Kent State Massacre, when students had been shot down and killed by police when they were demonstrating peaceably and unarmed, was fresh in people's minds, and when the group played *Machine Gun*, with Jimi's guitar sounding like actual machine-gun fire, it was tremendously moving and effective.

The audience reception was exceptionally strong as the group brought in the New Year, and included in their set a re-working of the Buddy Miles composition the now legendary *Them Changes*.

It was indeed a magical night, and many must have agreed with Bill Graham when he went on record as saying that 'the performance by Jimi and his Band of Gypsies was the best set of rock and roll music ever performed at the Fillmore East Theatre'.

*   *   *

Jimi himself was not so happy about it. His comments on the album recorded from the concert were:

'I was out of tune on some of the songs, and they were pressing me for the album, so here it is. I thought some of the things we did were pretty groovy, but I also felt that some of them could have been better.'

As usual, applause and public acclaim meant far less to Jimi than the satisfaction he felt when he knew in his own mind that the music was good; and so although the Band of Gypsies début had been heralded as a success, it wasn't musically gratifying or inspirational to Jimi himself.

Consequently, when he was asked to headline another concert with his Band of Gypsies soon afterwards, he only agreed with reluctance and because he felt that the money he would get from doing it would go a long way towards finishing the new dream-recording-studio, Electric Ladyland, which he had aimed at for so long.

'I felt,' he told me, 'that whatever I earned doing concerts would be that much less I would have to borrow and eventually pay back to the record company.'

This second Band of Gypsies gig, near the end of January (1970), was a Moratorium concert at New York's spectacular sports arena, Madison Square Gardens. The supposedly-ingenious concert organisers had got the idea, from Heaven only knows where, that a slowly revolving stage would be the answer to the complaints of many people who paid good money to go to concerts there, only to find that they wound up seeing stacks of amplifiers and perhaps the backs of the heads of the people they had gone to see.

The place was packed: a place used to hold everything from professional boxing to circuses, from basketball to ice-hockey matches, from Horse Shows to Roller Derbies, a place with its own bowling alley and a Hall of Fame above and the great Pennsylvania Rail-Road Station below. For Jimi Hendrix there was a crowd of some 19,000 screaming fans, waiting impatiently for the show to begin. I thought the great domed ceiling just might cave in from the rhythmic stomping of their 38,000 feet.

It has been said that someone gave Jimi a tab of acid that night, and that he took it just before he went on stage. Well, I can only say that I was there backstage and I didn't see such a thing happen.

I remember the expression I saw on Jimi's face as he followed Billy Cox and Buddy Miles—Buddy wearing his English-made boots of electric blue with white stars—out onto the stage. It was a look that I had come to know well: a look that Jimi got on his face when he didn't like something, or felt bad vibes. He told me later: 'Man, that fucking revolving stage was a drag. I would have just as soon been swinging from a tree trying to play.'

During the first number, Jimi broke a string, and I could see that he was hassled because the roadie was slow in getting one of his other guitars. So after struggling on through the first half of the second number Jimi walked up to the microphone and said 'Ah, I'm sorry but we just can't get it together' and walked off the stage.

19,000 people sat in stunned silence; you could, as they say, hear a chinch piss on cotton. They sat there for a brief moment and then filed silently out, understanding that Jimi had done what he had to do. That was the end of the Band of Gypsies.

When I spoke with Buddy Miles, shortly after Jimi's death, I asked him how he'd felt about working with Jimi.

'I was the recipient of good fortune,' he answered. 'I was honoured to play with Jimi when he became disenchanted with The Experience; I was just pleased to be a part of it when he wanted to try something new.'

And, he told me, he believed it could have worked out well.

'Bill Graham was reported to have said that the concert

where the album was cut, which was the début of the Band of Gypsies, in fact, was one of the greatest sets of rock 'n' roll he had ever heard.'

To what, then, I asked him, did he attribute the short life of the band?

'Well,' Buddy replied, 'I felt that Jimi was going through a very restless period, with a lot of pressures, both business and personal, on his mind, and that it was just one of those things. I mean, that's why he walked off stage at the Moratorium concert. That's why it broke up. Just one of those things.'

Jimi took things easy for a while after the demise of the band. He visited the Scene on West 46th Street, but he wasn't even into jamming much like he used to be. He was content to just sit and let the groupies surround him and then pick out maybe one or more, depending on his mood, and split with them and have a scene. It seemed like he still had to do something with his tremendous sexual energy; yet there were times when he wouldn't fuck a chick if she undressed in front of him and looked like Venus the Goddess of Love.

He wasn't making much music or much of a scene.

In May, the intended reformation of the original Jimi Hendrix Experience was announced, but in fact Jimi got in touch with Mitch in England again and started working again with him and Billy Cox. When he was asked about this arrangement, Jimi said:

'I had always planned to change the bass player. Noel is definitely out. Billy has a solid style of playing which suits me. I'm not going to say that one is better than the other, it's just that right now I prefer a more solid style. I'm not exactly sure how I feel about the Experience now ... it's a ghost now—it's dead like yesterday's flowers. I'm into new things now and I want to think about tomorrow, not yesterday.'

Still based in New York, Jimi started touring again with

Mitch and Billy, notably playing a concert at the Berkeley Community Theatre on 30 May, which was recorded and from which some numbers were used on albums put out after Jimi's death.

From there Jimi went on to Hawaii. He had never been to Hawaii before and was very happy when he was asked to do a concert there. After his arrival he felt that the concert had special spiritual significance when he learned that it was to take place near an active volcano. Jimi also told me:

'One day a flying saucer appeared and everybody that saw it was astonished that I knew exactly where it came from and why it was here. It was just part of the people from the supreme planet of material wisdom on a mission of peace and love.'

Jimi stayed on in Hawaii to make the film *Rainbow Bridge*, which opened in London, at last, in 1973, at the same time as the so-called biographical film on Jimi called simply *Jimi Hendrix*. The soundtrack album for *Rainbow Bridge* was recorded at various times and in various different studios, but mostly it was done at the Electric Ladyland studios on 1 July 1970, with Billy and Mitch as the basic line-up behind Jimi, augmented now and then by the Ghetto Fighters and Juma Edwards (vocal back-up and percussion respectively).

Four weeks later, Jimi played his last concert in America; and it is both ironic and significant that it took place in Seattle, Washington, where Jimi had been born; where it all began.

28 July 1970; Jimi Hendrix with Billy Cox on bass and Mitch Mitchell on drums. And as the group was due to go on stage at the stadium where the outdoor concert was being held, it started to rain—as if the sky was crying, showing its grief in advance of the impending tragedy.

Rain had not been predicted or expected, so a canopy had to be hastily mounted over the stage, while the impatient crowd of over 9,000 waited in the pouring rain. When the canopy had been erected the group emerged with Jimi dressed more flamboyantly than had become usual for him by this point in his career: bright yellow satin pants, a specially-made pyramid-sleeved shirt in violet, green, blue, white and rose. He looked, as someone remarked, 'like a psychedelic rainbow'.

Spontaneously, as the group came on stage, the people rushed towards him like he was a god—ocean-waves of humanity eager to baptise themselves in this happening. But Jimi began to play badly; painful sounds were emitted from the guitar that had no relevance to the songs the group were playing. He was lost as though he had no control; his body was contorted as if possessed by some evil demon; he was clearly in spiritual agony.

He became aware that rain-soaked confused faces, frowning disapproving faces, were staring at him from the crowd. Suddenly the vibes became so strong that Jimi said to the audience 'Fuck you! Fuck you!' And then just as suddenly, Jimi saw a smiling face, a little girl of about three years old in a yellow dress, looking at him. Smiling joyously, he returned to the microphone and said: 'I would like to dedicate the next song to the little girl over there in the yellow dress.' It was the first sign of joy he had seen in the crowd.

But the people were not responding. They could see that Jimi was very untogether. A few groups of people began chanting 'We love you, Jimi; We love you, Jimi,' and he responded momentarily to this sporadic chanting and began to play well—like the last burst of flame from a candle about to be blown out by a gust of wind.

Near the scheduled end of the concert, Jimi snatched his guitar from his back, flung it down onto the stage and walked off in disgust. He went over to a small group of relatives and friends standing in a semi-circle at the rear of the stage, stayed there for a few minutes and then, as rain-

soaked people were leaving Jimi walked back to the microphone and said: 'Is there anybody here from Garfield High
School?' A lot of kids yelled 'Yeah! Yeah! Yeah!' Jimi said
wanly, 'Far out.' It was a desperate old show-biz gimmick
for getting a response. Jimi said good-bye to his family and
friends and returned to New York City once again.

It was in the month after that—on 25 August, in fact—
that the official opening of Jimi's Electric Ladyland studios
occurred, and Jimi's dream became a reality.

In the planning stages of the studio, there had been a lot of
concern about the location chosen. The site was in the heart
of Greenwich Village on bustling 8th Street, one of the main
streets in the West Village. On one side of the studio there
is a theatre showing 'art pictures' of an original and un-
inhibited nature, and around the corner is the famous
Washington Square Park, a gathering-place for musicians of
all nations. Every Sunday, you can find a Greek band there,
a blues group, a folk group: almost any kind of music
imaginable, and with clusters of people either watching or
singing along in the festive atmosphere.

So it was an appropriate place for Jimi's dream-studio; not
least, it was fitting that Jimi chose to build it in the area
where he had spent his happiest hours in New York City.

The studio is also close to the Big Apple's counterpart of
the Speakeasy in London: a bar and restaurant called
Nobody's, where most of the musicians and heads and people
who are into rock go.

The front of the Electric Ladyland studio, built with red
brick, is somewhat rounded, distinguishing it from all the
other flat buildings on the block.

In every way, in fact, the whole dream-come-true seemed
fine and dandy.

Yet there had, of course, been serious problems. There
had, for instance, been a lot of worrying over the fact that
the studio was rather close to the 6th Avenue subway line,

because of the possibility of too much vibration from the rattling trains. However, Jimi was very relieved after extensive tests had established that the studio could be constructed in such a way that the subway would have no effect on it.

A more serious problem was the financial one, as far as Jimi was concerned. He was very distressed when it was pointed out to him that his financial affairs were in such a state that in order to build the studio in partnership with Mike Jeffries, he would after all have to borrow heavily from his record company.

Jimi told me : 'I know I have been spending a lot of money lately, but I have also been making a lot of money, and I was shocked to learn what my financial situation is. I had a lot of faith in the people that were handling my affairs—I trusted them. But there are definitely going to be some changes made.'

Yet in spite of his disillusionment at the state of his affairs, and the memory of the Seattle concert, Jimi had clearly been elated, looking forward to the grand opening of his Electric Ladyland studio.

Inside, the place is designed to give an atmosphere of being in space. As you enter the studio you must pass across an electronic eye barrier; then as you pass through the reception area you enter a passageway like a tunnel which takes you to Studio 1, the main studio. This tunnel/passageway is rounded and carpeted, giving you the feeling of being in a jet-plane. The main studio itself is a 32-track, with every electronic innovation that could be conceived of, presided over by top engineer Eddie Kramer. It also offers several different types of piano, a wide range of amplifying equipment and even drums (though most groups prefer to use their own drums when recording).

Jimi had wanted to provide all these special facilities because he remembered only too well the days when he had had no guitar and been forced to borrow an amplifier in order to make it to a gig. Later, after he had gone to England and done the Isle of Wight Festival, Jimi got in touch with me again and we talked for the last time together, and I remember him saying:

'I hope all of the musicians possible use my studio, because that is why I built it, so that musicians can have every possible innovation. I made sure that we had all the latest amplifiers, keyboards and other assorted recording equipment available without extra charge, because I remember, and it wasn't so long ago, when we first met and I didn't even have a guitar or an amp, and you gave me one. I wanted to do something for my brother musicians, all the beautiful people, each in their own way giving something of themselves for someone else.'

If Jimi had lived, no doubt his Electric Ladyland studio would have become one of the most popular on the East Coast, despite the reservations which Eric Burdon, for one, felt about it.

Burdon was unimpressed with the studio—but there are, as he explained to me—special reasons for that.

'I had bad feelings about it,' he told me, 'but that's because I thought that it was partly mine, really. Jimi knew it and I knew it; but we never discussed it because we were always into music. But I would never go down to the studio because the vibrations, for me, were just so bad: because I hated his manager so much—Mike Jeffries, that is.

'Mike Jeffries had brought The Animals to London in the first place. He got us a record deal and then systematically screwed us into the ground for every cent we got. That's who Mike Jeffries was. He also systematically screwed Jimi Hendrix into the ground too.

'When he and Chas both managed him, Chas was directing. Like, he was a *creative* manager. Good creative ideas. All the initial trips—like Monterey and all that—were all Chas' idea. Chas managed Jimi incredibly well.

'I also think he produced Jimi better than Jimi produced himself, in some respects. I think Chas knew what to do with Jimi's voicing. And with the mix, too. Whereas, when Jimi got to make his own mixes, he was a bit worried about his own voicing.

'But later on, Mike Jeffries took over the management— just because Chas couldn't, in the end, handle Jimi personally: because Jimi was getting sort of crazy. So Jeffries ended up *the* manager. And he was always at the studio.

'So I didn't bother going down there. I took a quick look inside there once. The soundtrack of *Hair* was cutting when I was in there.

'Maybe I'm wrong, but when you saw the squalor on that street and the way it was, and the studio was downstairs from it, man it seemed to me it was like being around Dien Bien Phu. And you know, I think Hendrix belonged somewhere else, like at least LA; or at least Denver or somewhere, or Seattle or somewhere. I would have figured Hawaii, with the volcanoes.

'But then again, New York's the business.'

At least the grand opening, on 25 August, was a joyful happening: a Gala Event. Everyone who was anyone was there, and the celebration was bathed in champagne and coloured with smoke from exotic lands, while well-meaning guests brought gifts in the form of pills of various colours and sizes. Everyone, including Jimi got stoned out of their heads—and that was the condition in which Jimi and his road-manager Eric Barrett got on the plane the next day, having had no sleep at all, to go back to England.

CHAPTER NINE

The final act

T he curtain was about to come down on the mortal existence of one of rock culture's greatest heroes. The stage was
set for the final act. Jimi Hendrix returned to England at the
end of August 1970—in the fall—as the leaves were changing
to the many colours of the rainbow; some dying, some
bringing new life into this world of perpetual death.

Still feeling the effects of the Electric Ladyland Gala
Opening party, Jimi and his road manager arrived at
Heathrow Airport, London, on the 27th, to headline what
Robin Denselow called 'the last great fling of British sixties
rock—the 1970 Isle of Wight Festival'.

East Afton Farm, Isle of Wight, on a cold damp night.
After all the soul-searching and inactivity that Jimi had
gone through, and with many music commentators feeling
that Jimi had reached the end of his creative powers, the
unspoken question at the festival site that night was: could
Jimi Hendrix really do it? Could he (with his group—Billy
Cox and Mitch Mitchell) again generate that magic excitement and stir the cosmic consciousness of the expectant
thousands?

It was almost three o'clock in the morning by the time the

other performances and all the delays were over and Jimi was ready to go on stage and tune up, and a mysterious fog had partially set in as Jimi prepared himself to go on and play what was to be almost his last concert ever. The huge searchlights which robbed the darkness of its heavenly-allotted time cast eerie shadows across a sea of tranquillity as the shapeless figures of the crowd huddled together under blankets in search of warmth and a renewal of energy after the weekend's toll of music and drugs.

The group went out onto the stage, shivered and played their historic set. Afterwards, Jimi described his feelings about the performance and the atmosphere to Monika:

'I felt cold and alone for a minute,' he told her, 'and then I felt all those people reaching up there on the stage to me. Then I knew that they hadn't forgotten me and I really felt good. They were calling out for *Purple Haze, Foxy Lady, Hey Joe* and all of the songs that I thought they'd forgotten.'

Despite the calling out, it was not the wild audience, nor the wild performance, that earlier Hendrix concerts had provided. Jimi's set was devoid of any visual fireworks, and there was quiet applause at the end of each number, rather than a frenetic tumult. It was as if they sensed some hidden message in his playing—sensed that his clock of musical life was winding down.

At least one other person sensed that too—an American girl who calls herself Joyce The Voice, and who had, that night, got herself backstage, had sung uninvited behind Leonard Cohen, and had then stood aside for Jimi's performance.

She told me:

'I was still backstage when Jimi came on to do his set—and something extraordinary happened. I was standing maybe six feet away from Jimi as he was playing, and the hassles of the Isle of Wight were really—you know, they'd really gone through the mill. It was the end of the festival practically. And then all of a sudden I had this flash—this white flash of energy came through me like electricity: like a shock. I could feel it in my spine, and I looked at Jimi and I knew. It felt like a scream of agony and of pain, and I realised at that moment that he was screaming out for help —desperately: and that he was going to die. And I wanted to kidnap him—to take him away from all the people that were invading him and, I felt, choking him—and take him out in the country and just clear away all those negative things that were around him.

'But I also knew in that same instant that I could not do it; that I was not strong enough; that I only saw and felt but I couldn't act.

'I don't think I was unique in feeling or knowing that Jimi was going to die: I think many people felt this. Such was his power. But no-one felt the strength to take him out of that web. It was almost as if we had to stand by and watch— not being together enough to reach out and help a friend.

'We couldn't: and it came out of him being the superstar and us just being the person on the side. At least, this is the way I saw it. And Jimi and I looked at each other with a kind of receptivity that I believe any human beings have when they truly see each other. No hallo; no words spoken; we just saw each other, and that was that.'

At the time, though Jimi's performance was good, many considered it a disappointment. Now, in retrospect, that assessment is perhaps changing. 'The music was excellent (even the Isle of Wight material . . .)' wrote Robin Denselow in the *Guardian* in 1973.

In a sense, Jimi seemed to be winding up his affairs. He had completed the *Cry of Love* album, except for editing and doing the final mix; he had phoned through to me in New York, as if to say good-bye, and appeared, in that last con- versation I had with Jimi, to have sorted out his ideas on the things and the people around him. He told me then that

Jimi relaxing after concert, 1968. *Photograph by Jan Persson*

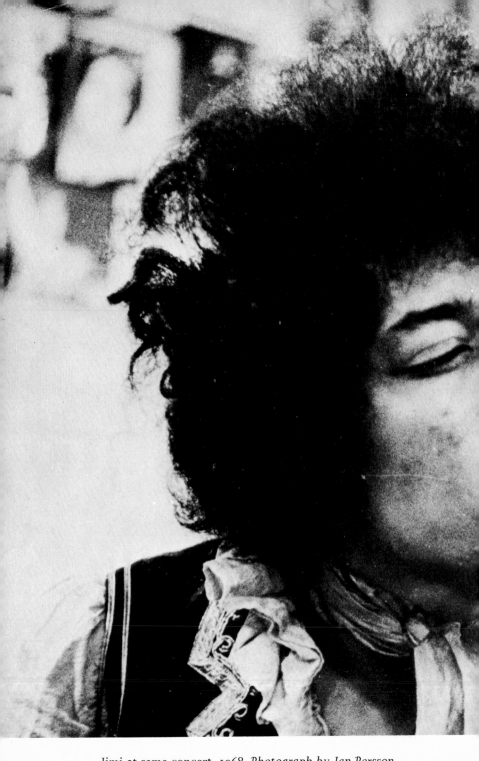

Jimi at same concert, 1968. *Photograph by Jan Persson*

Jimi and Mitch (*bottom left*) in full
musical flight. *Photographs of Jimi*

Hendrix by Jan Persson, photograph of
Mitch Mitchell by Laurens van Houten

Jimi mentally orbiting. *Photographs by*

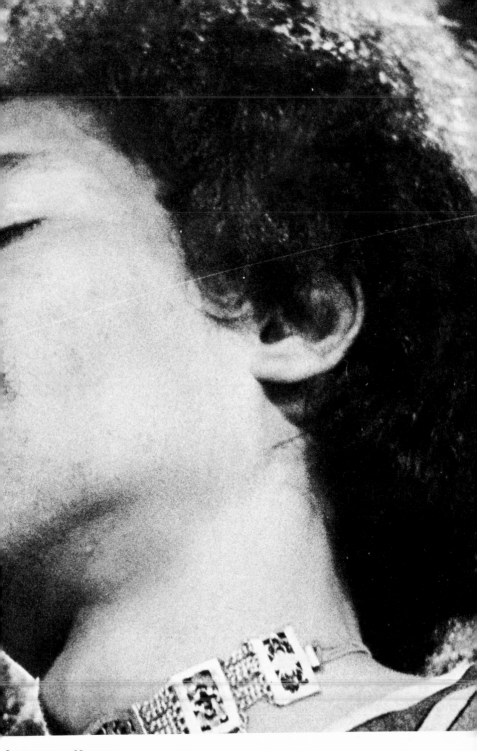

Laurens van Houten

Scandinavian concert – depths of his soul. *Photographs by Jan Persson*

he believed that groupies, who had been so much a part of his life as a musician, were 'the disciples of a musical religion, following it where- and whenever possible, giving vent to their feelings in a more honest way than many of our high and mighty moral pillars of this thing called a society : for this society is blind to the basic philosophies of life—love, peace and freedom'. And he told me too that he had decided what must be done to straighten out his financial affairs.

'I've just recently become aware,' he said to me, 'of vast irregularities in my financial situation, and I am going to get in touch with my lawyer in America and straighten everything out. The vultures have fed off me long enough.'

A short tour of Germany and Europe followed.

It was during this last tour, while Jimi was playing Berlin, that he was seen by Robin Trower, then lead guitarist of Procol Harum, whose comments serve to illumine what was happening around Jimi at that time. For Robin Trower believes that Jimi's performance was excellent—no sign that Hendrix was past his creative peak—that he was so good, in fact, that he went way beyond the comprehension of his audience : and that was obviously not a situation that Jimi, always passionately concerned to communicate with people, felt happy with.

Robin told me :

'It was the first time I'd ever seen him play. Up till then I'd been sort of avoiding him, because I always felt that when I did see him, I'd want to give up playing the guitar. I just knew that it was going to be "forget it", y'know? And that happened : I saw him and I did feel "forget it". I was in the dumps for a couple of months, especially when he died just about a week later. It had quite a strange effect on me.

'And then, Berlin was a strange gig. It was us (Procol Harum), and then Canned Heat, and Ten Years After, and then Jimi was on. And up until when Jimi came on everybody was going down better and better and better. And then when Jimi was on, the audience just wasn't there—they weren't digging it. I think it was above their heads, you know. I mean, I couldn't take in a lot of what he was doing and I'm a musician, a guitarist, so you can imagine what it was like for them.

'I was very very choked—because I felt very very annoyed at the audience. The band I didn't think played that well together but I felt he was the first real maestro I'd ever seen—a real maestro of the instrument; and just on that sheer fact alone I think that he should have gone down the best that anybody's gone down.

'So anyway, then I was walking up and down outside the dressing-room after he'd come off, and I was sort of saying should I go in? should I not?—and then I burst into the dressing-room all of a sudden and I said "Er—I've just gotta tell you, it was the best thing I ever seen"—which it was—and he said "Uh, thank you but uh naw!" and I just went woops, that's it, and walked out again.

'So that was the first and last time I met him. But I don't think he'd ever stopped expanding. And it's possible that, as good as the people he played with were, they weren't the right people for him to play with. I'm only saying it's possible, but it is a possibility that they weren't the right people to help him get it together best. But he was just so far ahead and up there. When I saw him in Berlin, I just looked: I watched it, I stood on a stand at the side of the stage and I watched what he was doing, but I couldn't bloody well take it in. I just didn't know what he was doing, you know? He was the first instrumentalist I'd ever seen that I could say that about. And so for a couple of months after that, well, I carried on playing but my heart wasn't in it. Because as far as I could see, the standards were set. He'd set the standards.'

The last gig of the tour, scheduled for Rotterdam, 14

September, was cancelled because, tragically, Billy Cox suffered a nervous breakdown and Jimi decided it would be best to send him back to the States. So Billy Cox was flown home to America and Jimi flew back, for the last time, to England.

Before this last sequence of poignant events, back in those earlier if no less unhappy days when Jimi had been in New York in seclusion, he had written letters to Monika in Dusseldorf. Then, after the Isle of Wight, when Jimi was back in Germany himself, Monika went, at Jimi's request, to find and move into a flat in London, where Jimi could join her on his return from that last brief tour. Monika obtained a flat in the very fashionable Lansdowne Crescent, in Notting Hill.

'Even though I had missed Jimi,' Monika told me, 'and was looking forward to seeing him, I had very strange feelings then. Feelings that I could find no answer for. It was as if I was myself and someone else at the same time.'

Jimi flew back into London and checked into the Cumberland Hotel at Marble Arch, not knowing where Monika had set up a flat because he hadn't communicated with her since Dusseldorf. But as destiny had planned it, and as Monika had hoped and dreamed, Jimi managed to get in touch with her through some friends.

During these last days, Jimi and Monika spent many hours walking among the trees and gardens in Hyde Park. Monika told me: 'Often Jimi would not speak for long periods of time, as if he was storing up and digesting his last direct communication with earth. During these times of silent meditation and spiritual self-consolement, he seemed to be communicating by some telepathic method unknown to earth inhabitants, and I walked with him silently, knowing and understanding his spiritual aloneness during these times.'

Monika also told me:

'Jimi and I had many specific and unusual conversations

in those last days. One question seemed to persist most in his mind, and it was a question he continually asked me. That question was: did I love him enough to die with him?

'I told him yes every time he asked me, meaning it from the depths of my heart—for Jimi had been my first and only love, and he was my whole life. He asked me what I would do if we made a pact to die together—would I just let him die and not die with him, and continue to live on earth: or would I die with him and take the spiritual journey with him.

'I always told him the same thing: that I would gladly die with him, for if he died life could hold no meaning for me.'

I asked Monika, too, about her paintings of Jimi. I remembered having seen them in her home in Dusseldorf. She is indeed an incredible artist, for she has captured the spiritual significance and scope of Jimi Hendrix on those canvases: she had to be truly inspired, and guided by a divine hand. Each painting is a world of knowledge within itself, in addition to being breathtakingly beautiful. I remember one painting in particular, which was so heavy and complicated that it took me a few days to feel I understood it.

The central theme of the painting is a cross, done in mist-like colours with a purple hue. The total colour theme of the painting is mauve, symbolising the coming-together and the blending of all the races in the world. Painted on the cross with Jimi—Jimi in vivid yet spirit-like appearance—are pictures of a cross-section of people who have had a profound effect on the civilisations of the world, past and present. They include Martin Luther King, Hitler, Chief Crazy Horse, Buddah and Geronimo. A very transitory touch is added by the fact that at the end of the human evolution of each of the subjects is an innocent baby of the subject's racial origin, dramatised by the presence of the cross and symbolic of all that is good. She had created this masterpiece with, and because of, Jimi's spiritual guidance.

When she spoke of these paintings, in connexion with those last days spent with Jimi, she told me:

'Jimi seemed to want peace and quiet in those last days, yet he seemed also to be trying to satisfy himself that at least some of the things that he'd envisioned would indeed be completed before he took his journey to infinity. He spoke to me about the paintings of him that he had told me to make. I assured him that they had been painted as he had directed.

'He particularly asked if the colours had been mixed according to his numerological instructions.'

It must have seemed, at this point, as if Jimi was about to get the legal wrangles between the Ed Chalpin/Capitol faction and the Mike Jeffries/Reprise faction sorted out for Europe too (as they had earlier been sorted out for the American market). The battle was about to reach the courts, it then appeared, and Ed Chalpin was in London, at the request of Jimi and his English representatives. I remember Ed telling me, before he left New York for London, that he was even hopeful of an out-of-court settlement.

In any case, two days before he died, Jimi was due to attend a meeting with the lawyers representing the rival sides.

But he didn't show up. He had left the Cumberland Hotel, where he was still registered, and failed to call round at Monika's flat. He had gone, instead, to a flatlet in the Fulham Road area.

Lorraine James, a twenty-one-year-old girl who works in the Chelsea Drug Store describes how he arrived on her doorstep:

'He was obviously high on drugs and he had a large quantity of cannabis on him. He was in a terrible state—highly nervous. He was on the coin phone-box in the building for hours, trying to contact people. One minute he was on top of the world and the next minute he was moaning about his backers and his financial affairs.

'There were two American girls visiting friends in the building, and Jimi made love to them both all through the night—until five in the morning. Then we all went off to Notting Hill and smoked pot at various pads in West London.

'Jimi was completely out of his mind. One man we met up with was so out of his mind with drugs that he jumped over the banisters of a house and was carted off to hospital with a broken leg. And when all this commotion happened, Jimi went mad and ran around the house shouting.'

All day Thursday Hendrix lay unconscious in the flat of a girl-friend in Redcliffe Gardens, Fulham. On the Thursday night, he returned to an orgy of drugs and girls, and finally made his way back to Monika Danneman's Notting Hill flat.

There, at 1.30 a.m., he made this 'epitaph' phone-call to Chas Chandler's number :

'I need help bad, man !'

These words rang out onto the answering machine in Chas Chandler's empty office. It was the last recording of the idol of millions, the prophet-in-chief of the drug generation.

The night before his death, Jimi and Monika returned to their flat at 8.30.

'I cooked a meal,' Monika said, 'and we ate and drank a bottle of wine. He drank more of the wine than I did, but he was not a drinking man. It was a very happy atmosphere. There was no argument or stress; we were just listening to music. About 1.45 a.m. he told me he had to go and see some people. I dropped him off at a flat, and then picked him up again just after three o'clock. We went back to the flat and I made him a tuna-fish sandwich.

'Then Jimi started to write what was to be his last message to the world : a song he appropriately called *The Story of Life*. When he finished with the song he told me to keep it no matter what happened, and not to give it to anyone until the time was right and the right person came along, and when it *was* the right time and the right person, I would know. And only then was I to tell anyone that I even had it.'

Monika continued: 'I had about twenty sleeping pills in a bottle that I had gotten through a doctor to help me sleep. They were kept in the bedroom, on my bureau. Jimi was in the bedroom alone, and on a sudden impulse I walked in. As I went in Jimi was pouring a large quantity of the pills into his hand. I grabbed the bottle from his hand, but he told me he was just counting them. I know now that he was just telling me that because he did not want me to know what he was going to do.

'Anyway, then Jimi had a small glass of wine and told me he was going to sleep. I sat on the edge of the bed and watched him until I thought he was asleep; then I took a sleeping-tablet myself. It was about 7 a.m.

'I woke up again at about 10.20 and I couldn't sleep any more. I wanted some cigarettes, but as Jimi did not like me to go out without telling him, I looked to see if he was awake. He was sleeping normally.

'Just before I went out I looked at him again, and there was sick on his nose and mouth. He was breathing and his pulse was beating—I checked it with mine and there was no difference. I put my shoes on quickly, grabbed my coat and ran across the street as quickly as I could.

'When I returned and approached the door of the flat, with my key in my hand, I sensed something was wrong. The door stuck this time, as it sometimes did, and I became very frightened. Finally I managed to get the door open, and when I rushed into the bedroom, even before I looked at him, I knew something was terribly wrong. There was only one lamp burning in the room, because I had turned the ceiling light off after I thought Jimi had gone to sleep. The lamp cast this eerie glow; there was a hush in the room as though time had stood still.

'My first impulse was to try to awaken him. I shook him again and again, frantically. I felt his face; it was cold. His lips were slightly parted and they had a purplish tint.'

Monika hoped that, in spite of her worst fears, Jimi was perhaps just sick.

'I prayed that some miracle would happen,' she said. 'I thought of calling the hospital but discarded the idea because I felt Jimi would be angry if he received undesirable publicity. I had not yet noticed my bottle of sleeping tablets, but then I saw them on the table beside the bed, and there were nine pills missing.

'I picked up the phone to call someone, to get some advice. When I reached a friend of mine and Jimi's, they quickly advised me to call the hospital regardless of the consequences.'

Monika called St Mary Abbot's hospital, but although the ambulance arrived very quickly—though it seemed like an eternity to Monika—it was already too late. Jimi was pronounced dead on arrival at the hospital.

The date was the 18 September 1970; Jimi was just twenty-seven years old.

The inquest was held on the 21st, and the pathologist, Professor Donald Teare, stated that the cause of death was suffocation from the inhalation of vomit due to barbiturate intoxication.

He pointed out that there was no evidence that Jimi Hendrix had been a drug addict, and commented that 'Hendrix bore no stigma of drug addiction—no needle marks.' Monika, feeling that her life too had just ended, said: 'He was very happy before I went to sleep. As far as I know he did not take any pep tablets, but he did mention he took some cannabis at the flat where he went to see the people.'

An open (undecided) verdict was recorded.

CHAPTER TEN

Flashbacks and aftermaths: In from the storm

This seems the right point in the story for me to relate Jimi's own views on life, death and eternity, just as he explained them to me. This is what Jimi told me:

'Both worlds, the present material world which we are all now in, and the eternal spiritual world, which is the only world where eternal life and total happiness are possible, do exist.' The one, Jimi said, was as real as the other, and 'as long as you do not live according to the ways of the god-like planet of supreme wisdom, you will suffer death and life in that order, and be reincarnated until you live in such a way as to be accepted as spirits of eternity.'

He also said:

'There is in our material world a planet of superior material wisdom that possesses all knowledge possible in this material world as you know it. It is possible for science to advance to such a stage that it possesses part of the material knowledge of this supreme planet of material wisdom.

'But since, by predestination, the material worlds are destroyed periodically, it is doubtful that even with science's rapid advances in technology that they can obtain enough knowledge to reach, or even communicate with, this planet of supreme material wisdom before man's greed and his other inadequacies cause him to destroy himself, thereby necessitating the material world to begin again as it has done so many times in the past.

'The materialistic planet of supreme wisdom is staffed by people not unlike people of your world but possessing all knowledge possible in the material world. Messengers from the *spiritual* world are sent periodically to these material worlds to guide them in their wisdom.'

I believe that Jimi Hendrix had been a messenger. Throughout history, there have been many prophets—saints and other divinely-guided men—who communicated with us in ways prescribed by the times. Some were believed in, some killed through man's profound ignorance and man's fear of the unknown. Jimi Hendrix was loved and respected for his contribution to the world of music, but his real purpose has not been understood. His message is in the lyrics of his songs and wherever his music takes you.

Hence it was that while Jimi made efforts, near the end, to leave things in order in the material world where he had been for so short a time, the last days of his life on earth were spent in preparation for his journey to spiritual eternity. Hence too Jimi told Monika that through her paintings she would 'communicate to the world my deep concern and eternal love for it'.

And Jimi had once said:

'People still mourn when people die, that's self-sympathy. The person who is dead ain't crying. When I die I want people to play my music, go wild and freak out, and do anything they wanna do. I don't want nobody to be sad. Sadness is for when a baby is born into this heavy world—and joy should be exhibited at someone's death because they are going onto something more permanent and something infinitely better.'

The complexities of Jimi's personality, and of his feelings in those last weeks of his life were manifest in other ways too. People had felt that he had deserted Britain; yet it was to Britain that Jimi finally returned in search of tranquillity and peace. People thought that he had flown back to Britain to do the Isle of Wight Festival simply as a fast way of getting a nice little stash of bread (he was paid £12,000— around 30,000 dollars—for appearing) and had thereby shown a mercenary arrogance; yet it was equally true that Jimi had always loved festivals for spiritual, not monetary, reasons: and there had been not a trace of arrogance on Jimi's part when, on the Wednesday night of the week he died, he had sat in with Eric Burdon and War, who were performing at Ronnie Scott's Soho club.

Eric himself told me exactly what happened:

'At that time, I think he was holed up in his hotel-room and he wouldn't speak to nobody or nothing. He was really blue-edged then. But he came down, first on the Monday night, and asked to play. We'—Eric Burdon and War—'played there for a week, and he came down on the Monday night: and he was out of his brain. I don't know what he was on. He was down on something, though. I thought it was smack and he was down on it, but it was probably Mandrax or something. But he was really the opposite of on top of the world—under the world, right?

'He said, "I wanna jam." And I said, "Well, come back tomorrow night. You know, put your suit on, bring your guitar with you; be smart and we'll jam." And he said, "Yeah, you're right." And he did. Wednesday night he came down and he was immaculate and straight as a dye. He brought his axe and he jammed. I guess that was the last time he played.

'And after that I said, "You know we'll get together," and he said, "Yeah, OK." And he just disappeared with the groupies. He went out of the door with the groupies: sank into the groupies. And that's the last thing I saw of him, man, just waving good-bye.'

There was nothing the least bit arrogant about that.

Neither had Jimi's attitude towards the people who had guided his career ever been simple and straightforward, as we have already seen. Jimi often felt that he just didn't know whether to trust them or not, and didn't know whether they had his well-being at heart even when he felt that they *were* looking after his finances properly. In this connexion, I remember particularly one story Jimi had told me, and which demonstrates his puzzlement vividly. It was the story of one of the strangest and most incredible incidents that ever happened to Jimi, and like so many strange events in his life, it happened in London.

'I wanted,' Jimi told me, 'to do a double-album for my next release, and I was promptly told by the management that there wasn't enough public demand for a double-LP, and that it was their intention to release a single LP. I couldn't understand that because every LP that had been released had become a best-seller. All of them had become Gold Records.

'Anyway, those were just part of the things that were on my mind as I walked along this quiet street, alone with my thoughts. And then suddenly, as though out of nowhere, my thoughts were interrupted by this screeching of brakes and the simultaneous opening of a car door—and before I realised what had happened I found myself forcibly abducted by four men. I was blindfolded and gagged and shoved rudely in the back of a car. I couldn't understand what the fuck was going on as I lay there sweating with someone's knee in my back.'

Because Jimi was a person who lived every day to try and make others happy, and was always ready to help rather than hurt people, it seemed to him like some senseless nightmare.

'I was taken,' he continued, 'to some deserted building and made to believe that they really intended to hurt me. They never did tell me *why* they abducted me. The whole thing seemed very mysterious, because after a while I realised that if they really had intended to hurt me they would have already done it by this time.

'And the whole thing seemed even more mysterious when I was rescued by these people supposedly sent by the management. They really effected a story-book rescue.'

Jimi never did decide whether this weird episode had been engineered by his management itself for publicity reasons.

In any event, publicity based on lies and distortions pursued him even after death. When the news first came through that Jimi was dead, and before the coroner had pronounced as to the true facts of how Jimi had died, the media were screaming out headlines and stories that he had died of a heroin overdose.

They were quick, too, to sensationalise the comments made by Eric Burdon concerning Jimi's death. As one newspaper reported it:

'A startling claim that pop star Jimi Hendrix's death was "deliberate" was made by one of his closest friends last night. It came from pop star Eric Burdon when he was interviewed on the BBC-TV programme 24 *Hours*. Burdon, singer with a group called War, said: "He used drugs to phase himself out of this life, and go someplace else." Burdon claimed that the American guitarist knew how to use drugs, and added: "Jimi realised that he was being artistically stifled ... Hendrix realised that to correct this would kill him artistically anyway ... That's the way Jimi was and Jimi just existed at the time he felt it was right." '

And another publication blared out with the news that according, again, to Eric Burdon, Jimi had left behind for the girl in whose apartment he died what Burdon called 'a suicide note' which was a poem several pages in length.

'The poem,' Burdon was reported as saying, 'just says the things Hendrix has always been saying, but to which nobody ever listened. It was a note of good-bye and a note of hello. I don't think Jimi committed suicide in the conventional way. He just decided to exit when he wanted to.'

Mike Jeffries was quick to deny any suggestions of suicide, and issued this statement from his office:

'I don't believe it was suicide. I've been going through a whole stack of papers, poems and songs that Jimi had written, and I could show you twenty of them that could be interpreted as a suicide note.'

What that 'suicide note' in question was, of course, was the song that Jimi had written in Monika's presence at her flat on that last fateful night—the song he had told Monika not to reveal until the right person came along—the song called *The Story of Life*.

The days following Jimi's death were unreal for Monika Danneman herself. Her brother, Herbert, tried to shield her from the publicity-hounds, giving this statement to the press in the hope that they would then leave his sister alone:

'Monika was in love with Jimi and is distraught at his death. She had known him for about two years but she had only been in London for about six weeks. And Jimi had told her that he did not want people to be sad if he died. He wanted everyone to be happy.'

But the reporters would not leave Monika alone; her life in those days was a maze of trying to dodge them all; and they were everywhere, everywhere she turned: trying to catch her, trying to get her to say things that would make good copy. In the end, a merciful friend managed to sneak her out of the flat where she had been living with Jimi.

That friend was Eric Burdon. Afterwards, he told me how it happened:

'Well, she was pretty much bombarded by press people and everything. And that morning, like everybody just descended on the whole scene and just started ripping everything off, man. Everything. It was weird. So she just spent a few days with us—because I was working on the road at the time, so we just inserted her in the group. And kept her in the middle of the group, so that nobody could get to her.'

So Monika at last escaped the harrassment which had only added to the pain of losing her first and last love. 'For me,' she said bravely, 'Jimi is not dead; his spirit is still with us. It is just the body that has gone away.'

Yet she could not escape entirely. She had to remain in London until after the inquest, and in the end, she became too embittered and angry over the false reports and rumours circulating about Jimi to keep silent.

'My love for Jimi,' she tried to explain, 'was something deep and personal. For those reasons I have refrained from talking about our relationship. It was an intimate thing between us, and not to be shared by the world. But this week I have been shocked and stunned—because Jimi has been put down, even by many of his so-called friends. Now I feel compelled to answer, because Jimi isn't here to defend himself and I must do this for him, and for his memory.

'I am certain that he was not a drug addict, nor an alcoholic, nor a sex maniac, and I shall tell the Westminster Coroner on Monday all I know ... The real Jimi behind the stage façade was a very sensitive, compassionate and shy person, who genuinely believed in the message Love, Peace, Freedom and Brotherhood he tried to give the world.

'We discovered we had close affinities with one another through our mutual love of art. Six weeks after our first meeting, Jimi asked me to live with him, but at that time I didn't believe that he could have any real feelings for me.

Like the rest, I was fooled by the wild stories about him.

'Wild? Jimi was the most sweet and tender man anyone could ever meet. Everyone took advantage of him because he was so kind. I soon realised how sincere Jimi was. Of course he had been around and had other affairs—the pop world is like that. Perhaps it was because I was not a groupie who was pursuing him, but I managed to find the real Jimi Hendrix, and his heart: the heart that no-one seems to have discovered.' Monika continued to try to counteract the lies with these words:

'Jimi lived for his music, and he was sick of the rest of it all. He told me many times how groupies would get into his hotel rooms and wait for him in his bed until he arrived; and Jimi would get his road-manager to throw them out.

'He also told me about his experiments with drugs at a time when many pop stars were also curious about smoking pot and trying out acid. But Jimi was never hooked on drugs, and in all the eighteen months we were together there was not one occasion I can recall when I saw him produce any.

'So many people were around him—but never near to him. Basically he was a very lonely person. Often he told me he did not know where he would be unless I was there with him.

'Much has been recorded of the last four days in Jimi's life and most of it is untrue. I was with him all those four days, every moment except for one hour on the night of his death, when he went to Marble Arch for some business discussions. When he returned he was perfectly happy and he was looking forward to going to America to finish a new album. He'd even booked his hotel in America, and his air passage, and he'd telephoned his recording studio in New York to let them know he was coming.'

Perhaps Monika was being over-zealous in her lone attempt to protect Jimi's memory from the prying and distorting of the media, because that account doesn't quite fit in with all the facts that have emerged as to Jimi's last few days; and nor does Kathy Etchingham, who perhaps was the one who knew Jimi best, give the same assessment of Jimi's private tastes and habits (as we shall see later on in this chapter). Yet Monika was trying loyally and conscientiously to direct the attention of the press to Jimi's essential goodness, so that in spirit—in the important things—Monika was right and truthful.

'I shall always remember,' she finished by saying, 'our last night together, when I cooked spaghetti bolognaise and we drank a bottle of wine over dinner. It was our last moment of happiness.'

Monika comes from Dusseldorf, where she grew up pursuing two careers, ice-skating and painting, until an accident cut short the first of these and so led her to concentrate on the second. It was shortly after that accident that Monika first met Jimi Hendrix. After his death, Monika invited me to spend a week at her parents' home, where I was able to see all her remarkable paintings of Jimi, and to talk at length to her about the Jimi she had known and loved well. She was understandably more informative than she had been to the press :

'From the very beginning of Jimi's career,' Monika told me, 'I had always been a big fan of his; and even though then I had never met him, I always felt something strange and different, that I couldn't understand, when I listened to his music.

'He had played here in Dusseldorf before, but for some reason I had been unable to go. I have a very good male friend here, who knows a lot of popular rock groups, and he had met Jimi at a concert in Germany. And then one day this friend asked me would I like to go to a concert in a town nearby, where The Jimi Hendrix Experience would be playing. I accepted the invitation, feeling that at last I would be able to see for myself if the strange secret feelings that

I felt every time I heard his music *was* just his music, or something beyond. I had spent most of that day painting, as usual, but I had sensed that something was about to happen that would change my life.

'When we arrived at the concert, the place was already so crowded that I wondered how we would ever be able to find our seats. But we did, and suddenly the lights dimmed, and I felt a cold shiver and leaned forward to the edge of my seat. As the stage lights came on, Jimi was standing there as if him and his white guitar were one.

'He looked so majestic, and I wondered for a moment if this was really happening or whether it was just a beautiful dream. Jimi began to play and the sounds of his guitar seemed to be carrying me with him, and he began to communicate with me about things I never knew existed.

'As the first half of the concert ended, my friend somehow managed to get us backstage, and finally he was able to reach Jimi. I hung back, because I didn't want him to think that I wanted to meet him for any other reason than admiration of his talent. I felt really funny when I saw he was looking at me.'

And with good reason. Jimi told me his side of the scene, sometime later, in these words: 'I saw her standing there, with her beautiful blonde hair down to her shoulders, and man, a real strange and exciting feeling came over me—oops, here I go again! She looked so good, I just wanted to go over and ... y'know, but I thought I better just be cool for now.'

'Then,' Monika continued, 'my friend introduced us, and I was a bit shocked because Jimi said right away could I come to his concert the next night. It was quite a few miles away. I told him I wasn't sure but I would try, and he said he'd be very happy if I would try to make it.

'That night, that next night, I felt he was playing just for me. He looked at me and our eyes found each other; Jimi smiled at me and I felt I had been lifted to the sky.

'But I decided to leave before the concert was over, because I felt I wanted time to see if what I was feeling was real, or if it was something that would pass.'

Jimi told me about this same evening:

'As I got ready for that concert, I wondered if Monika would be there or was it just to be footsteps in the wind that would blow past with the next moon. But I had felt, back at the hotel room the night before, that destiny had intended my meeting with Monika, and that she would share a part of my life with me, and that she would inspire me.

'As I went on stage that night, I wondered "Will she be here?" and I knew that if she came, I wouldn't consider our meeting an ordinary encounter. Then I went on to do our first number, and there she was. I didn't see anyone in that packed audience except Monika.

'I assumed that she would wait for me after the concert, because I felt like we already had something going on between us; all we had to do was, ah, put it together, you know? I couldn't hardly wait to finish the encore. I looked out into the audience. She wasn't there!'

For a moment, a feeling of disappointment swept over him, and then he told himself that Monika would probably be waiting for him backstage. As he hurriedly worked his way through the backstage crowd, accepting congratulations and signing as few autographs as possible, he began to realise what he had already somehow sensed. Monika really had gone.

'This puzzled me, you know,' Jimi told me, 'because this was one of the first times that a foxy chick ever slipped through my fingers—now how about that!'

Jimi was really struck. He continued his tour of Germany somewhat saddened, and returned to England feeling that he had left a part of himself in Germany; as he put it later : 'I knew that I could not feel complete until I saw Monika again.'

He tried to stay busy, and as he was scheduled to return to the States soon afterwards for another tour, he began to try to write new material. But he found that he couldn't come up with new ideas as easily as he had in the past.

Meanwhile Monika, in Jimi's absence, had grown to realise that the feelings she had for him were real, and she decided to write Jimi a letter explaining why she hadn't waited after that concert, and how she felt.

She had to wait a long time for a reply to that letter, and was afraid that he had perhaps forgotten all about her; but it was simply that Jimi had been moving around such a lot that it took a long time for Monika's letter to reach him.

When it did, Jimi was touched and happy, and sure within *himself* that there was something very deep and meaningful between them. He answered her letter at once, telling her his feelings.

Shortly after that, Jimi returned to England with Monika uppermost in his mind. He called her up in Germany, and as they talked, they both realised that they were plugged into destiny. It could not be long before they met again.

And then shortly after that phone call, one of Monika's friends told her he was going to London on business; so Monika decided to go along.

Monika takes up the story again from there :
'I arrived in London feeling that I was going to have a rendezvous with happiness. That night, my friend and I went down to the Speakeasy at about midnight, and we were both a little hungry so we ate there.

'As we were eating and talking, I suddenly realised that someone was standing behind me. I turned around and there was Jimi. I gasped in surprise and before I could say anything, he pulled me to my feet and kissed me.

'I was really embarrassed and surprised, but I felt very close to Jimi in that moment when he kissed me; and then we just stood there looking at each other for what seemed like an hour, though I guess it was probably only a few minutes. Then Jimi said, "I have been looking forward to seeing you for a long time, and I couldn't be happier"—and then he realised that someone was sitting with me, and he whispered to me "Is that your boy-friend?" and I smiled and explained.

'We spent many hours together that night, talking and getting into each other's heads, discovering lots of fascinating things about each other. And Jimi told me he wasn't a bit surprised to find out that I was an artist.'

After that, for the rest of the time that Monika was in London, the two of them were inseparable. It seemed to Jimi at this point in his life that at least he could be happy with Monika, even if other things weren't going his way.

When Monika returned to Germany she began to paint her very sensitive and very beautiful pictures of Jimi, which she loved doing because she felt able to bring out in her work the many beautiful qualities that she saw in Jimi and which perhaps others did not see, and because it kept her close to him in spirit. She was encouraged in her work by her mother, who would often go and pick up materials that Monika needed, while Monika worked continuously—often right through the night—not wanting to break the spiritual spell that surrounded her when she was creating a painting of Jimi.

'And then,' Monika told me, continuing her story, 'I got to thinking of how I would like to go back to London and rent a flat there where I could paint and be close to Jimi when he came back to England. And what happened then was that he wrote to me, telling me that he soon would be back in England, and asking me to go over and get a flat ready.

'So that's what I did—and the rest you know,' Monika concluded, avoiding the memories of her hounding by the press in the days immediately following Jimi's death.

It wasn't only the press who were intruding and closing in at this time. There were also, inevitably, a number of business people on the scene, anxiously prising open the financial situation created by Jimi's death.

There was much speculation about a possible secret will. One publication reported that:

'London lawyers have ordered a detailed investigation into the affairs of the pop star Jimi Hendrix, who died under mysterious circumstances. At stake is a fortune worth at least £200,000, with many more thousands of pounds to come from record royalties in the future. No will has been found in America, and a New York court, with Judge S. Samuel Diflaco presiding, has appointed a lawyer, Mr Henry Steingarten, who acted as adviser to Mr Hendrix, as administrator of his estate. Now, enquiries are being made to see whether Jimi made a will in Britain, or perhaps brought one with him from America ... A legal source commented: "We do not know yet whether there is one. The estate will take some time to settle, because there are record company sales which take time to accrue." Meanwhile lawyers in America have begun talks over million-dollar insurance policies taken out on Hendrix's life by the Hollywood film company Warner Brothers.'

The report went on to note that under New York State law, in the event of their being no will the entire estate would pass to his father, James Allen Hendrix, in Seattle, since

Jimi, whose mother had died in 1958, had never married.

Meanwhile, while that particular legal hassle was being investigated, the other big financial battle—the dispute between Jeffries and Chalpin—was also continuing. There had still been no settlement of this dispute as regards Britain and Europe by the time of Jimi's death, yet it had seemed that such a settlement was imminent. Ed Chalpin had flown into London on the Tuesday—15 September—for the meeting which Hendrix had failed to attend. Asked by the press as to the outcome of that meeting, Chalpin said: 'We discussed royalties and' (ironically enough) 'the future of Jimi Hendrix ... I showed proof that I signed him in 1965, more than a year before he came to England. He came back in 1967, after The Experience had been formed, and recorded again for me, with Curtis Knight. The issue about royalties must now be settled in an English court. I tried for three days to get to Jimi, but I was blocked. And then I was shattered to hear of his death.'

Yet the reaction to Jimi's demise was not all hostility and rumour-mongering, sensationalising and predatory manoeuvring. There were few people who felt able to follow Jimi's own exhortations to be happy rather than sad; but many, many thousands of people were affected deeply, fans and other stars alike; people who had never known the personal side of Jimi, and people who had known it well; people who had idolised the star, and people who had loved the man. This compassionate, human side of the world Jimi had departed did manifest itself, and did counterbalance all the mud-slinging and the grabbing.

The news of Jimi's death was broken to Mick Jagger, one of Jimi's closest friends, while the Rolling Stones were in the middle of a European tour (they had reached, ironically enough, Monika Danneman's home-town, Dusseldorf) and Mick spoke for many besides himself when he said: 'I'm absolutely stunned—we all are. I cannot at this time talk about the death of such a very great friend and great musician. I'm absolutely shattered.' And the night of the day that Jimi Hendrix died, The Grateful Dead, appearing at the Fillmore East Theatre, dedicated their five-hour set to him, while it was reported all over the world that musicians and artists in every field of entertainment dedicated songs and performances to him, and made mention of his death to their audiences, and expressed their deep shock and sorrow at the news.

Many of the major rock music radio stations played his music non-stop in tribute the day he died, and even so-called middle-of-the-road stations in America which were not known for playing rock music or even recognising the existence of rock musicians broke precedent and played some of Jimi's recordings.

Mitch Mitchell expressed his final thoughts about Jimi this way:

'Jimi was an inspirational musical leader and musical brother, and a person endowed with unlimited talent. He is still here with us; he will never die.'

Eddie Kramer, master engineer at Jimi's dream-studio, Electric Ladyland, told me:

'Everyone here loved and respected Jimi and we feel as if he is still here, because the studio was him and he was the studio.'

Miles Davis told me:

'There was a fairly general consensus, you know, among the leading jazz musicians who had taken the opportunity to get into Jimi Hendrix, that had he taken a strict jazz direction with his music, which he was certainly capable of doing, that Jimi would have certainly been one of the jazz giants.'

Pete Townshend told me:

'My theory about Jimi—it might be a bit pretentious to

come out with one—was that everything happened to him in such a big way, and in such a short time, that it was like an explosion. He lived his whole life squashed up into twenty-six years, and he got more out of life than most people ever get in. And as far as I'm concerned, he had done it. He'd done everything that there was to do. He could have added some more trimmings, but how could he ever have surpassed what he'd done? His life was like a trip in a way: he'd had the hump, right?—the explosion—and he was gently and slowly coming down. So I think that if he hadn't died, maybe he would have mellowed out.

'I think probably he would have surprised a lot of people. He was much more of an all-round musician than a lot of people knew. I mean if you sat in a room while he banged about on acoustic, he could play really pretty guitar.

'See that's the thing about Jimi. A lot of people think of that wild man, and they forget how he could play really pretty guitar, you know?

'But anyway, now, it's a tragedy for the music business that there isn't a Jimi Hendrix around playing music.'

Eric Burdon told me:

'The black people in America still yet, have got to wake up to who he was. And it's all on tape and it's all on film and there's still time to do it. And I think it's going to happen.

'People are going to get hip to what he was into. But it just takes time, that's all.'

And when I talked to John and Yoko about Jimi's death, John told me he thought Jimi had been 'the Pied Piper of rock —an innovator—and one of the most influential figures of the era: totally original'. I asked him how long he thought Jimi and his music would be remembered, and he answered:

'He will be remembered as long as music is a part of our lives—and I'm sure that that will be forever.'

Many more affectionate tributes poured in from saddened friends and artists all over the world.

Jimi's publicist, Michael Goldstein, who had to send out obituary notices to the press, said:

'What can I say? Jimi will certainly be missed. People out there remember his performances, his attitude. I remember his smile, his giggle, his wink ... his whisper. Those are things that related to me personally. I remember whimsical conversations we had ... being on the road for a year. It's like losing a member of your family. As far as what it will mean to rock and roll or to the public, well I just can't think about that.'

Eric Dolphy, a friend of Jimi's, said:

'His death really hit me hard, and Coltrane. I don't think the world treats artists the right way anyhow. I don't think they ever have.'

Don Van Vliet (Captain Beefheart) said:

'I don't feel he knew how much he could have done, cause he was so good. I felt that he was one of the only good ones on that instrument. He wasn't afraid to experiment. But those drugs, man, that hard stuff, that should have gone out after Charlie Parker, don't you think? That's no way to expand your mind. I don't know why anybody ever thought it was. All it ends up to be is hard stuff; hard stuff, hard life. But Jimi, he was just so good. There was so much he could have done.'

Charles Lloyd, another of Jimi's friends, said:

'He was a young dude, and I had hoped that in his lifetime he wouldn't have to pay the same dues as people like Prez (Lester Young) and Bird (Charlie Parker) and Billie Holliday had to pay. But he was sweet and soft and had a vulnerable nature. I don't know what took Jimi to that place, but its pretty painful to me. What can you say? We live in this fucked-up world. People who make music somehow have to be protected. I don't know quite what that means but maybe we shouldn't be subjected to that kind of thing.'

Robin Trower, then lead guitarist of Procol Harum, told me:

'He was so underrated. People talk about him and say yeah, he was really great: but they don't know; they don't *know*. They missed it, I think; they really did miss it. I think in about twenty years' time people may really catch on. His scope was so wide, y'know? His scope was endless.'

And Eric Clapton said:

'His death is a tragic loss to anyone who listens to music and something indescribable to me as his friend.'

Kathy Etchingham must have felt especially the loss that Jimi Hendrix's death had brought. She had perhaps known Jimi more closely and intimately than any other girl who had ever come into his life. Yet she managed to talk about the man she had loved with great clarity of insight and with unswerving frankness, at this most difficult time:

'I'm sure it wasn't suicide,' she told one reporter. 'Jimi had lots of troubles but he wasn't the sort of person to take his own life. It must have been an accident.'

She went on, in this interview, to talk about the Hendrix so many people didn't know, who could be violent one minute and then placid the next, and who could fill himself up with drugs one minute and be perfectly normal the next.

Did he drink? the reporter asked.

'He was on fruit juice when he first came here, but that soon changed: he could drink up to a bottle and a half of whisky at a single session,' she admitted.

What about drugs, the reporter wanted to know.

'It was hash that turned him on; from there he went onto cocaine, and eventually, heroin,' Kathy confessed.

And women?

'He'd have intercourse with up to four women in the same bedroom,' said Kathy. 'He has illegitimate children in Sweden, America and Germany.'

If the reporter was motivated by a professional instinct for scandal, I think it has to be said that Kathy was motivated simply by a desire to be honest and to communicate what she had experienced and felt in being around Jimi. She wasn't playing the media's games, even though what she told them was exactly what they had hoped to hear.

'When I met Jimi for the first time,' Kathy explained, 'he was very quiet and drank only soft drinks. But a few years later he was psychologically hooked on drugs like coke [cocaine] and pills and LSD. Recently his hair was turning grey and he was losing it. All along he was forced into this life, but all he wanted was to be a musician. He didn't want to do anything but play his guitar, but it was such a struggle.

'I married someone else, with Jimi's blessing, last November, but I still kept on seeing Jimi. He told my husband that he still loved me, and although it sounds strange, the three of us agreed that Jimi and I could still have a scene together. Jimi had money troubles and desperately needed to confide in someone. He had a different person to confide in for every problem. I was his love and his money confidante.'

On the Friday night, within a few hours of hearing of Jimi's death, Kathy and her husband and the heads of Jimi's record company went out to celebrate his death. 'Celebrate', that is, in the sense that Jimi had told people to do. Kathy explained :

'We went out and had a lot to drink—we got blind drunk, which may seem rather strange, but this is what Jimi would have wanted. He often told me that when he died he wanted everyone to have a good time; he didn't want anyone to mourn his death.'

Of Jimi's sexual exploits, Kathy said :

'He had an incredible sexual appetite and would often sleep with three or four girls in the same night. He used girls like some people smoke cigarettes. He was the one who invented the name "Band Aids" for the groupies who hung around him constantly. He wouldn't have to go looking for them; they came looking for him. He had a great choice. Many times he told me casually about the times he'd been with four women in one big bed. He would talk of this quite nonchalantly. He wouldn't even recognise the girls the next night.

'One night after a concert in Manchester, I even found him in the ladies' loo with a chick. She meant nothing to him, and it meant nothing to me—apart from the fact that I had to tell him to hurry up or we would miss the train back to London.

'Jimi did everything to excess. He would drink a bottle and a half of whisky—an American quart bottle—in an evening. He would start when "Coronation Street" came on the television, and by midnight he would be ready to go out for a meal, and start drinking wine. With drink as with everything else, he only felt he had enough when he collapsed.

'Before I met him he was working in bands touring America on one-night stands, virtually penniless. He had two scars on his wrists, and he told me that one night in a friend's bathroom he was so desperate that he cut his wrists with a razor-blade. He failed to cut the artery in one hand, and the friend found him and took him to the hospital. He cursed his friend because the hospital bill only made his position worse. But that was when he was just a struggling down-and-out musician.'

Ranging further through her memories of Jimi, Kathy went on:

'You could never predict the next thing he would do. One moment he would be quiet and gentle and the next moment he could become a different person. Without provocation he would smash up a room, no matter whose house he was in, and hit anyone who interfered, man or woman. We used to have terrible fights over nothing.

'One time he fractured my nose in three places with his foot. I got him back a few weeks later when he was sleeping, by hitting him over the head with a frying pan which was under the bed. When he woke up he didn't know what had happened, and I pretended I was asleep.

'After his bouts of violence, he was always very sorry for what he had done and would take all the blame on himself.'

However, Kathy said, that didn't stop the same kind of thing happening again. In fact, nothing ever really stopped Jimi from spontaneously doing what he wanted.

'Jimi was totally free like the wind. To have tried to possess him would have been like putting a wild bird in a cage.

'He didn't want to die, I know, but he wouldn't be unhappy about it. He went as he would have wanted : stoned in bed with a beautiful girl and without any pain.'

Kathy talked, too, of Jimi's penchant for filming, and even for recording some of his sexual exploits on film.

'He went really crazy about cine-filming,' she said. 'He bought a lovely camera and projector and sometimes he'd just lean out of the window and film people walking across the road. He had a thing about taking films of really fat women, or skinny ugly ones; then he used to show the films and laugh at them. He would also get friends of his to film women running around naked in his room. Often, though, these films were blacked out by the processing people if they got a bit way-out.'

Kathy described the way Jimi would recklessly ravage his body with all the narcotics in the junkie's book. 'He always wanted to experiment. It was the same with songs, musical instruments and drugs. When I first met Jimi he smoked hash, though not often; but then came LSD. Jimi would take it in liquid on sugar or even blotting paper. He would often take acid trips on his own. It was in America that he started taking cocaine. He was frightened of the hypodermic needle, so he kept to snorting his coke. Sometimes his nostrils would be red sore. I tried to get him off drugs altogether, but he couldn't.'

Kathy also explained : 'Jimi was never in-between. He was either in a very good mood or a very bad mood. Normally we would stay up into the early hours of the morning— usually down at the Speakeasy. Jimi would sleep until the early afternoon; then he'd get up and have a cup of tea. Sometimes he'd be hungry and I'd make him fried chicken and rice. Often Jimi would just lie in bed for a couple of days on end, not interested in anything. He'd be out cold— not even interested in sex.

'He hated telephones, and at one time wanted to have them all cut off in the flat. He rarely answered the phone.'

Kathy described how she became used to meeting up with girls who had slept with Jimi in different parts of the world. 'Chicks from Sweden, Germany, all over the place, would turn up at the flat asking for Jimi—girls he'd met on tour, had a night with and given his address to. I think it shook them a bit to find me there, but I'd be quite nice, give them a cup of coffee and show them out. Then I'd tell Jimi later about it, and he'd say "Oh, thanks," so casual—it meant nothing to him, it was his way of life. Sometimes there would be notes pushed under the door saying "If you don't do something about it, I am going to take out a paternity order against you".'

And Kathy confirmed, too, other people's impression that Jimi Hendrix would indeed, depending on the circumstances, take any emotion to the outer limits.

'I will never forget,' she said, 'being backstage one night and seeing him smash his guitar. It was quite fantastic—he was livid with fury. I saw his face as he turned his back on the audience : he really hated that guitar! You could see he was going to kill it; it was frightening. I couldn't bear to look at his face again when he was smashing the guitar. When he came back into the dressing-room he just sat down in silence.'

Such was the complex world of Jimi Hendrix as Kathy knew it.

When, later, Kathy visited me in London, we talked at greater length. Kathy reminisced about her life with Jimi, sometimes jumping back and forth from incident to incident, talking freely and openly about the good times and the bad, as she sat in my room, sipping one of her favourite wines. What follows, then, has no rigidly consistent chronology, but it is the truth behind what was probably the longest-standing relationship between Jimi and any one girl:

'When I first met him, Jimi didn't hardly drink at all, just an occasional beer or wine. He didn't even seem to smoke hash till he came to England. I think he'd smoked grass and on rare occasions I think he'd sniffed a little coke when he'd been at the right place at the right time, where someone with a lot of bread was passing it around (which wasn't often). Cocaine was very expensive in America then; about forty dollars a spoon.

'I feel that Jimi probably started drinking more because of me, because he was my man and I liked drinking. And Jimi didn't really have it so easy in England as a lot of people think. I can remember many times when he first came over here when he wasn't sure if he could ever get it together.

'You know, I knew Jimi was a genius guitar-player, but I didn't really like his music. And I told him so. He even tried to teach me to play guitar. He would hold his long fingers down on the guitar strings and I would try to strum: but he and I both agreed that I was hopeless.

'Jimi really taught me a lot. I mean, because when we first started living together, I was very young and kind of wild and I didn't really know the meaning of being one man's girl. Even after I moved in with Jimi I still got dressed

Billy Cox – base guitarist in Band of Gypsyes, replaced by Noel Redding in the Experience after break-up. *Photograph by Laurens van Houten*

(SE 3)SEATTLE, OCT.1--(AP)--FRIENDS OF THE LATE POP SINGER JIMI HENDRIX CARRY HIS COFFIN FROM CHURCH THURSDAY AFTER FUNERAL SERVICES. THE PALL BEARERS INCLUDE HERBERT PRICE, LEFT, HENDRIX'S VALET; DONNY HOWELL, BEHIND HIM;AND EDDIE RYE, FRONT RIGHT. HOWELL AND RYE WERE FRIENDS OF HENDRIX WHEN HE WAS A YOUTH IN SEATTLE. OTHERS IN PHOTO ARE NOT IDENTIFIED. (AP WIREPHOTO) GR 1970.

Picture of me standing in front of Electric Lady Studios. *Photograph courtesy of Allen Liffman Photography*

Inside Electric Lady Studios, this is the big studio 'A', with all the ultra-modern recording equipment. *Photograph courtesy of Allen Liffman Photography*

Top: Ed Chalpin, Hendrix's first producer, Monika Danneman and myself examining snake ring given to Monika by Jimi. *Photograph by Annette Elbe*. *Below*: Me with Zeus, my current group

and went out every night just like I had always done. Jimi put up with it for a while, and then one night after he got fed up with me running wild, he locked me in the bedroom and wouldn't let me out. When he did come to let me out, hours later, I'd fallen asleep. But after that, and after many hours of patient explaining on his part, I finally began to realise how I was supposed to act, both as a woman and when I was living with someone that I loved. So for that and for getting my head together and making me more mature, I really have Jimi to thank.

'Then after Jimi had been over here six or seven months and had begun to be popular, things started happening that I didn't like very much, though there was nothing I could do about it. His managers tried to hide it from the press that we were living together. They didn't think that it was good for his image, to have it known that he had a regular girl-friend. So I used to have to hide in the bedroom when he was being interviewed in our flat. And that made me feel very uncomfortable.

'It took Jimi and me over a year to find a proper flat, and by that time he had really reached success. The place we finally found was really convenient because at that time everybody was going to the Speakeasy and we got this flat right around the corner. So we could just walk around there every time Jimi wanted to go around and jam or if we wanted to just go there and eat or anything.

'Then, you know, the first time that Jimi went back to the States, in 1967, I wanted to go with him because it was to be the longest period of separation for us since I had known him. But because it was his first trip over there with The Experience, it wasn't possible to take me, and Jimi promised that he would let me come over the next time he went to the States.

'Anyhow, to go back a bit from then, you know Jimi was very jealous in those early days. He had these fits of jealousy;

he didn't want me to have anything to do with any other guys. I remember one night specifically, in the Bag O' Nails; Jimi and I were there and I left the table to go upstairs to phone a girl-friend, and I was gone a little longer than he thought I should be gone, and he came upstairs raging mad because he thought I was talking to some guy on the phone. He snatched the booth door open, snatched the phone out of my hand and started beating me on the head with it. I thought he was going crazy and I began to scream—and at the same time, I was trying to have a go at him. But even though Jimi was very skinny, he was very strong and he was definitely too much for me. And then just in the nick of time, like as if it was in some James Bond movie, John Lennon and Paul McCartney were coming into the club, and they saw what was happening and so they pulled Jimi off of me and took him over to the side and cooled him down. That may have been the first of our many fights.

'But one of the most frightening things to happen to me was an incident concerning this chick. Jimi and I were asleep in the bed one morning and the first thing I remember was looking up and seeing this white guitar coming at me. Jimi immediately threw himself on top of me to absorb the blows that were coming at us—I must give him full credit, he did try to protect me. I don't know how long this continued but the girl finally stormed out of the room with the guitar that she was supposed to have bought for him.

'After that little exhibition was over, Jimi had to figure out some way to get his guitar back because that was the only one he had at that time, and he could hardly afford to buy one. So Jimi got in touch with her and with some smooth-talking managed to persuade her to bring the guitar back : but her conditions were that Jimi had to get rid of me.

'And so Jimi told her he would—so that she'd bring it back. Then he told me to wait in the lobby so she wouldn't see me when she came to return the guitar. Now I saw her when she came in the lobby that day, but I was sitting where she couldn't see me. Jimi told me afterwards that he'd had to make love to her to quiet her down and pacify her, and that she'd got into the room that day she attacked us with the guitar by giving some money to the maid.

'But then as she was leaving, when she'd given the guitar back, she saw me. I'd got tired of sitting in that one spot and I was kind of walking around and before I knew it, there she was and she'd spotted me. Man, she really freaked out! There was nothing dull about life as long as I was with Jimi.

'In fact, things got heavier. Specially when I did get to America. Things were getting kind of heavy between me and Jimi then. I don't know why, but it seemed like every time I came to America, after a while Jimi would start feeling that he didn't have as much freedom as he wanted, and he would start making plans to ship me back to London.

'But this one time I wasn't ready to go, so I just moved out of this hotel I was staying in with Jimi, and moved into another. I had this girl-friend who was living with this guy in a real plush hotel. He had a suite and the whole bit, and also they were really into cocaine, and I quite liked that. And if I was gonna split for a while, I knew Jimi would find out about it and when he found me, I wanted him to find me in a situation where I was living as good as I had been with him. Seems funny, doesn't it? But that was the way I was think-ing. Anyway, my girl-friend came over one day, and I was really down that day. I probably would never have split on my own but when she arrived and saw how down I was she suggested I move in with her and her boy-friend; so we just gathered all of my things together and we split over to her hotel.

'But I still knew that what Jimi would do would be, when he found me, come in and say what the hell, and then he'd most likely slap me around a little bit and then try to ship me back to England anyway.

'Yet there again, you know, I had gone to New York at Jimi's invitation and at his expense, and Jimi had made all the necessary arrangements for my comfort. He even saw to it that I had a car to drive me around when I needed it. He even had one of the guys he trusted to take me out when he was out of the city. He would really have been uptight if he'd known that the guy he told to take me out was really digging me!

'I was very curious about Harlem—and that was a heavy scene too. One night I got this same guy to take me to Smalls Paradise in Harlem. Man, those black chicks in that club didn't dig me being there; but I could tell by the way that all the black guys were looking at me that they didn't mind. But suddenly I looked around in that club and saw that I was the only white chick in there—and I got a little nervous. And then I had to go to the ladies loo, and I never really expected any hassles, but this is what happened: just as I came out of the toilet, and was standing in the mirror combing my hair, four black chicks came in, and I kind of figured they came in to start something because none of them used the loo and they were just looking at me, so I decided it was time for me to split. I started to go out the door and one chick stuck her leg out to trip me. But then I just quickly stepped over her foot and man, I was out of there before they could do anything else. We got out of that club in a hurry: I'd seen enough of Smalls Paradise.

'That stuff happened a lot. I had another bad experience like that in New York. Jimi had been recording all day in some studio—I believe it was the Record Plant—and Jimi called the hotel and told me to come down there. It was about nine p.m. when I arrived, and just before I got to the door to go in the studio where Jimi was actually recording, I had to go up some steps, and there were these four *white* chicks waiting for me. I guess they were American groupies and they'd probably been in the studio, and as near as I can figure it out, they'd heard that I was coming down there and they didn't dig it because I was Jimi's chick; so they must have decided to wait outside and do me.

'Well, before I knew what was happening they had knocked me down the steps and started kicking me everywhere. I don't exactly remember everything, but the next thing I knew, I was in an ambulance—and I remember thinking how strange their ambulances are over there because they have glass everywhere and everybody could see right in, and I felt really funny.

'In some ways Jimi was very naïve—like for instance, he was always being ripped off with bad dope by this guy by the name of Rock—and in some ways I was very naïve myself. I remember this one incident when instead of following my own mind, I was completely dominated by someone else—this supergroupie, Devon. Devon almost brainwashed me into suicide. Devon was a very hip black chick, a real supergroupie who knew everyone, and she must have sussed out right away that I would be influenced by what she said. At this point I hadn't seen Jimi for a while, and even though I wasn't really a jealous person and I knew Jimi was seeing a lot of other chicks, I knew also that Devon still wanted Jimi, and for some reason when she started telling me all these things that Jimi had been doing with all these other chicks, I got really uptight. I remember Jimi was doing a recording session that night and I was in the hotel room on my own. I felt really down, so after Devon split I just grabbed a bottle of sleeping pills.

'I don't know how many I took; all I know is that it was a lot, but anyway Jerry Sickles was sent back to the hotel room to pick up a bass or something that they had forgotten —and if it wasn't for the fact that he was sent there to pick up this musical instrument that they'd forgotten and needed at the recording session, I probably wouldn't be alive today. Because when he came in the hotel room, I was lying on the floor, and they said I wouldn't have lived much longer. Anyway, Jerry rushed me to the hospital and they pumped my stomach out. And Jimi was really mad when he heard about what had happened, and when he came and saw me he just called me a stupid bitch and a lot of other nasty things.

'He was a strange guy. You know, he could be like that and yet he could be so protective. Like one of the worst times I remember was when we went over to this black power leader's pad. Jimi was invited over there to this guy's house because they said they had some really nice dope, and so naturally Jimi took me along. And then it was really weird when we got there. I could tell right away that they didn't like white people and the way they looked at me when I walked in there with Jimi—it was obvious they didn't dig me being there with him. Jimi sensed it too, but he didn't want to just turn around and walk back out: Jimi was like that, he didn't want to hurt their feelings. So we stayed long enough to have a few smokes and then Jimi thanked them politely and we got the hell out of there. Jimi said "Phew!—those were some heavy bad vibes," and we both breathed a sigh of relief when we got out of there. I'd been scared stiff: yet I knew without a doubt that Jimi would never have let anything happen to me.'

Finally, Kathy told me about the last time she saw Jimi alive.

'The last time I saw Jimi was the day of the night he died. It was in Kensington Market. He was with that blonde chick, so I didn't say anything to him. He didn't even see me. I had planned to see him later that night. Maybe if I had spoken to him and he'd seen me, he wouldn't now be dead.'

One day I was walking into a shop in the King's Road with the intention of buying something flash and quite by accident or was it destiny, I met Marianne Faithfull. Wearing a black floppy hat that almost covered her angelic face, she began rapping about her first meeting with Jimi.

'The first time I saw Jimi was quite by chance. I was on my own one night and I went into this small club for a drink and Jimi and the Experience happened to be playing there. It was one of their very first gigs in London and they had not yet begun to attract the massive crowds that were soon to discover them when the word got around. They were literally playing to empty tables and chairs. I sat down on the floor and there was kind of an instantaneous visual communication between Jimi and I. Neither one of us said anything, but for one brief moment we had a telepathic spiritual conversation. Jimi somehow sensed that there was at least one person who would really be listening to him and he responded as though filled with sudden flow of electrical energy. I was amazed at this black, sensual, musical god and when he started playing the guitar with his teeth, that was really something! He was too good to be true. I stayed the whole evening drinking in and digesting his musical vibrations. I went again the following night and said to myself that it was just a matter of time until Jimi Hendrix would be recognised as the musical giant that he was. He just couldn't miss.

'For three nights in a row I went to hear him, each time being turned on, and becoming more and more tuned in to what he was into. I had a lot of friends in the music business who, I knew, would really dig him if they knew what he was all about. But for three nights I decided to have him musically for myself, and it was beautiful. Then I got on the phone and told all my friends about Jimi. After that a lot of the well-known people and really hip heads began to go and see him. Not only was he a brilliant guitarist, he was very sensual and visual—an unbeatable combination.

'At the time when Jimi first came to London the whole scene was different than it is now. Being a pop star was really something then and the stars were genuinely welcome wherever they went. But now things have drastically changed. I did something for Jimi that I rarely do for people, and that is to stick my neck out. I organised a party in Jimi's honour at the home of one of my friends one night after we had all been to see him perform. I took a big chance because I really didn't know how it would come off, but he was really beautiful and everybody really dug him.' Marianne smiled as she reminisced and then continued.

'It was a strange and beautiful relationship that Jimi and I had. Nothing physical ever happened, but the beautiful tension was always there. We had somehow gone beyond the entrapment of the physical and reached the upper echelons of real communication. I think in some ways Jimi was lucky to have exited when he did. I think he knew it was time to go.'

I also spoke, after Jimi's death, to Pete Townshend and Eric Burdon, and asked them for *their* speculations about Jimi and drugs. Specifically, I asked them whether they thought drugs had helped, hindered or been irrelevant to, Jimi's creativity—yet both their answers inevitably ended up as reflections on his death.

Pete Townshend told me:

'I know Jimi was pretty much of a wild man when it came to dope, as a lot of people in the business are. It's like how easy it is for a business man to become an alcoholic. When he arrives at a meeting they give him a gin.

'I know I used to get a lot of buzzes from dope, and I don't think there would have been such an amazing Jimi Hendrix without dope. It's really hard to say. I saw him on one occasion when he was straight and he was just an ordinary, nice, easy-going guy.

'But then, I think more happened inside his body and brain and soul when he walked on a stage than just drugs. There was more chemistry in him than drugs when he walked on a stage. It's not just as simple as drugs either supplementing what he was doing or what he was, helping it, adding to it or taking away. He was what he was; there was some magic in him, doing it. And of course, just like everybody else, doing the dope added another dimension to that, I suppose—and it's still steaming along, I think.

'I see a lot of people get fucked up—that's really what worries me, you know. I mean, to look at it fairly clinically, look at Jimi's death. That's something which a lot of people get, that thing about boozing and then taking sleepers, right? Very very ordinary straight people get that—they drink too much, they take a sleeper; then if they're sick in the night, they just choke, y'know. This is a very common thing, it happens all the time.

'Janis Joplin died in exactly the same way, and quite possibly Brian Jones died in the same way. Suffocation, and just being so out of it that you just can't fight it.'

Eric Burdon's reflections were rather different:

'I think,' he told me, 'that drugs have to be got into perspective in anybody's life in society today, period. I don't think Jimi Hendrix could have written what he had written if he hadn't dropped acid. But there again, if Jimi Hendrix hadn't been born, he would not have been able to drop acid, if you see what I mean. You know, it's which comes first, the chicken or the egg?

'I've heard people say that Jimi's mind was blown by acid and what it revealed to him. You have revelations. If you can handle revelations, you can handle them. If you can't or if something else is revealed to you, you have to do what you have to do. And I think that's what Hendrix did. Everything was a tool to him. Guitar was a tool. Music was a tool. Drugs were a tool.

'I think he played his life as well as he played his axe. And I think he died at the time he wanted to. As coolly and as calmly as he came into the world.'

Those first days after Jimi's death passed slowly; but at last the inquest was held. The true circumstances of how Jimi had died were announced and the papers had to take back their tales of a heroin overdose. In another place and another time, Jimi had said: 'When I die I want to be buried by the Thames River, in England. Don't bury me in Seattle, it's too cold and damp there. And I want people to put on all my old clothes and dance on my grave.' But Jimi's body *was* flown to Seattle and buried there a week after the inquest. And though no-one felt like dancing on Jimi's grave, someone did (as mentioned earlier) have the heartlessness and greed to steal the gravestone paid for out of Jimi's father's hard-earned money, not very long after the burial.

Jazz star Miles Davis was one of the few personalities who attended the funeral for Jimi, and his reasons for being there were very beautiful. He told me afterwards that he had thought many strange thoughts as he'd boarded the plane for Seattle. He took his trumpet with him because he felt that a musical send-off was in order and he felt he knew somehow that Jimi would have wanted him to bring it, and that even if circumstances prevented the jam that Jimi had said he wanted when he died, he would at least have the trumpet in spiritual readiness.

The jam session was *not* held, at the request of the Hendrix family, so Miles Davis, understanding and respecting their wishes, just contented himself with saying a verbal 'so long' to a friend and brother.

Understandable though it was that the family should have requested a quiet funeral, it remains probable (and equally understandable) that Jimi, at the last, would indeed have wanted the jam he had often talked of. Perhaps Jimi would have felt regretful, too, that by an ironic twist of fate, the funeral service held for him was at that same Dunlan Baptist Church he had been thrown out of as a child for wearing 'improper dress' and to which he had, all those years before, vowed he would never return.

Yet Jimi Hendrix had always been a person who accepted

and respected fate; and he was also a person who did not harbour negative feelings of resentment.

And thus it was appropriate that the album he had completed, but for the final mix, just before he died—the musical message he bequeathed to us all and which was released in December 1970—was entitled *Cry of Love*.

Jimi Hendrix's cry of love has indeed reached out and touched the world.

I have to end this book by giving Jimi himself the last word. What follows, then, is a final collection of stories from within *the* story of Jimi Hendrix.

The first one, actually, is too short and too rhetorical, on the surface, to be categorised as a story at all. But the pulse and pressure of feeling, of Jimi's feeling, that it reveals, tells us vividly, despite its brevity, what it had been like for Jimi to live out his superstardom. And in giving us that vivid picture of a whole aspect of Jimi's life, it is a very big story indeed:

THE FIRST STORY: If I'm free ...

'Me, free?! If I'm free well it's because I'm always running. I tend to feel like a fugitive from public opinion. They want to know about these girls, kicking people in the ass, doing the power to the people sign. I cut my hair, they say why'd you cut your hair, Jimi? It was breaking up. Where d'you get those socks? What made you wear blue socks today? Then I started to ask my*self* questions: did I take too much solo? Should I have said thank-you to that girl? I'm tired—not physically but mentally. I'm gonna grow my hair back. It's something to hide behind.'

I was on my way for a walk across Hyde Park one day, and at the bottom of the stairs, just before I stepped out into Kensington High Street, a young guy walked up to me and said 'Are you Curtis Knight?' I told him I was and he said,

'I hear you are writing a book on Jimi Hendrix, and I have something to tell you.'

The next evening, he came around and I listened to what he had to tell me; and what follows is his story :

THE SECOND STORY : The Mystical Experience of Mark Paternostro.

'I am a painter, and I found Curtis Knight because I felt I had to, to tell him this story.

In my paintings, I had gotten into the air brush. When I work with it, it is like working with my hands in rhythm. The way I semi-theorised it, it's like just an immediate flow of consciousness without really thinking about it—kind of a subconscious push. And I had done one painting of Jimi Hendrix, one pastel of Jimi, and I knew his face inside out. I had built the canvas and filled the brush with paint. I started at one end of the canvas just to incorporate the natural rhythm based quite a bit on musical rhythms.

So what that led to was, I'd get to the point where I would reach my natural vibrations. So I laid in the first layer in a flowing wavy-type background and as I added my colours then I'd get to a certain point where I'd sit back and look for images within the positive and negative space inter-changeably.

On the left side of the canvas I got just the flash of a space-boat. I continued and as I reached the right upper corner of the canvas I realised that there was an image of Hendrix there. And there was one other image in the painting, which was another face, which I took as myself. The thing I thought strange about it was that when I started I had no idea what I was going to paint.

As I look at it now, it seemed like I wasn't really doing it : either it wasn't me doing it or it was part of my subconscious. And when I'd finished it I really hadn't comprehended what I'd done. I had a glimpse of what it meant, that's all; but in the weeks that followed, as I gave it consciousness, it turned out to be a foreshadowing of my future experiences.

I knew that there was a certain path that I had to look into.

After that it just worked out that I was going to England, which is where it all became clear what the painting I had done really meant. The spaceship was like a symbol of the knowledge that I found in England, and from the spaceship —the spaceboat—I found out the books that Jimi Hendrix had read. And from that knowledge I seemed to reach the essence of what I thought Jimi's purpose was in the end. In one way his purpose was the beginning of the coming of greater light on earth. From where I look at it, it seems like he was here, he realised that he had to do something, he did it and then he left.

The effect of his guitar on consciousness! ... I can now see the ultimate potential of electrical guitar energy—the musical vibrations used as a neutraliser of the thought organ, thus freezing the mind to proceed to further and deeper concentration. Certain musical energies seem to be of far greater impact when concentrating totally on them and then looking into the third eye, at the precise intersection. The loss of your body, free-falling into space; total hallucination, travelling on an electrical vibration at the speed of light.

I had spent months and months listening to his music after his death. The particular song I listened to was *Earth Blues*. In that particular song I really comprehended where he was at, and it was a time for me of trying to find my own spiritual essence.

I was awed by the fact that he was addressing himself to God. And what happened on one particular occasion—and only one—was that I must have had some doubt in my mind that there was a God, and near the end of the song the word Love was in my mind : and then I heard him say, "What do you think God's about?" '

The final story, again in Jimi's own words, is a moving eloquent expression of at least a part of Jimi's philosophy, starting with his vivid description of drugs and their related meanings, as he explained it to me:

THE LAST STORY: Timeless Light to the Edge of your Soul
'Drugs are in general a very hip and mysterious experience. First I want to say probably a lot of people have heard of black magic, or voodoo, and references to people being possessed. Well, drugs can be all of that, and sometimes more. They can also be less than nothing.

I have heard that for a long time doctors have been giving people who were incurably ill shots that gave them all kinds of vivid dreams and sent them into various states of ecstasy and made them forget about the horrible pains they might be having, and in a lot of cases where they could have died at any moment, they were given a resurgence of life by these drugs.

Also people who participate in certain types of ancient rituals have communicated in some mysterious way with some of the timeless vibrations in the wind, and have become possessed by perhaps what they were in another life, or what their character suggests they really are; or sometimes they have been known to become pigs, chickens or anything that the true spiritual soul dictates.

Some people look to catch a reflection of pure sunlight and find madness. Or is it profound wisdom that is too heavy perhaps for society to comprehend? Maybe the people that are in institutions should be out and society that condemns their so-called irrational behaviour should be locked up.

LSD is the ultimate in mind-expression psychedelic drugs. I was into it to see what was happening with it. Sometimes I saw an inter-relation of spider-webs holding the world together; sometimes celestial figures dressed in divine gold would try to stop people from digging for evil—those lovers of evil who magnified their evil by attaching significance to every evil experience they perpetrated.

One time on a trip I saw the walls breathing—and the principal feature of that experience is that you and what you are experiencing are inseparable.

I saw people running around frantically trying to escape from themselves and being swallowed up by all of the colours in the rainbow.

On bad trips sometimes I saw monsters too horrible to explain, and a drug-induced psychic horror is not easy to handle.

I have to say that if you become dependent on drugs for better experiences, they destroy your spiritual potential. A state of alertness is really essential.

To enjoy a concert, for an example, the audience should put just as much into enjoying the concert as a musician might do in playing for them. You can be possessed by a voo-doo of sounds.

In Biblical times, fasting was a method of preparedness for the acceptance of the divine spiritual light. But truth, peace and love are the true paths that we should walk. Not the drug trail, because that only leads to a dead end.

If you are true believers, destiny will show you the way.'

A Jimi Hendrix Discography

Compiled by John McKellar

1. OFFICIAL COMMERCIAL LPS

'Are You Experienced' (September 1967) (Gold Record)
Reprise RS-6261 (USA)
Track 99 2407 010 (GB)
Polydor 184 085 (GB)
Also available as Backtrack 10
A Yameta Production, produced by Chas Chandler
The Jimi Hendrix Experience
Mitch Mitchell, drums; Noel Redding, bass

US version:
Side One: *Purple Haze; Manic Depression; Hey Joe; Love or Confusion; May This Be Love; I Don't Live Today*
Side Two: *The Wind Cries Mary; Third Stone From The Sun; Foxy Lady; Are You Experienced*

GB version:
Side One: *Foxy Lady; Manic Depression; Red House; Can You See Me; Love or Confusion; I Don't Live Today*
Side Two: *May This Be Love; Fire; Third Stone From The Sun; Remember; Are You Experienced*

'Axis: Bold As Love' (March 1968) (Gold Record)
Reprise RS-6281 (USA)
Track 99 2407 011 (GB)
Polydor 184 110 (GB)
Also available as Backtrack 11
Produced by Chas Chandler; engineer, Eddie Kramer
The Jimi Hendrix Experience
Mitch Mitchell, drums; Noel Redding, bass
Side One: *EXP; Up From The Skies; Spanish Castle Magic; Wait Until Tomorrow; Ain't No Telling; Little Wing; If Six Was Nine*

Side Two: *You Got Me Floatin'*; *Castles Made Of Sand*; *She's So Fine* (by Noel Redding); *One Rainy Wish*; *Little Miss Lover*; *Bold As Love*

'Smash Hits' (June 1968) (Gold Record)
 Reprise MS-2025 (USA)
 Track 613 004 (GB)
No production credits
The Jimi Hendrix Experience
Mitch Mitchell, drums; Noel Redding, bass

US version:
 Side One: *Purple Haze*; *Fire*; *The Wind Cries Mary*; *Can You See Me*; *Hey Joe*; *Stone Free*
 Side Two: *Manic Depression*; *Foxy Lady*; *Crosstown Traffic*; *All Along The Watchtower*; *Red House*; *Remember*

GB version:
 Side One: *Purple Haze*; *Fire*; *The Wind Cries Mary*; *Can You See Me*; *51st Anniversary*; *Hey Joe*
 Side Two: *Stone Free*; *Stars That Play With Laughing Sam's Dice*; *Manic Depression*; *Highway Chile*; *Burning of the Midnight Lamp*; *Foxy Lady*

'Electric Ladyland' (August 1968) (Gold Record)
 Reprise 2RS-6307 (USA)
 Track 2657 001 (GB)
 Polydor 184 183/4 (GB)
Produced and directed by Jimi Hendrix
Engineers: Eddie Kramer and Gary Kellgren
The Jimi Hendrix Experience
Mitch Mitchell, drums; Noel Redding, bass
Help from our friends and passengers includes:
On *Rainy Day* and *Still Raining*: Mike Finnigan, organ; Larry Faucette, congas; Freddie Smith, horn; Buddy Miles, drums. On *Voodoo Child*: Stevie Winwood, organ; Jack Casady, bass. On *Long Hot Summer Night*: Al Kooper, piano
 Side A: *... And The Gods Made Love*; *Have You Ever Been (To Electric Ladyland)*; *Crosstown Traffic*; *Voodoo Child*
 Side B: *Little Miss Strange* (by Noel Redding); *Long Hot Summer Night*; *Come On* (by Earl King); *Gypsy Eyes*; *Burning of the Midnight Lamp*
 Side C: *Rainy Day, Dream Away*: *1983 ... (A Merman I Should Turn To Be)*; *Moon Turn The Tides ... gently, gently away*
 Side D: *Still Raining, Still Dreaming*; *House Burning Down*; *All Along The Watchtower* (by Bob Dylan); *Voodoo Child* (Slight Return)

'Band of Gypsies' (May 1970)
 Capitol STAO 472 (USA)
 Track 2406 002 (GB)

Polydor 248 005 (GB)
Recorded live, Fillmore East, New York, 1/1/70
Produced by Heaven Research, recorded live by Wally Heider; Remix
engineering by Eddie Kramer
The Band of Gypsies
Buddy Miles, drums; Billy Cox, bass
  Side One: *Who Knows; Machine Gun*
  Side Two: *Changes* (by Buddy Miles); *Power of Soul; Message to
  Love; We Gotta Live Together* (by Buddy Miles)

'The Cry Of Love' (December 1970)
  Track 2408 101 (GB)
  Polydor 2408 101 (GB)
Produced by Jimi Hendrix, Mitch Mitchell and Eddie Kramer
Mitch Mitchell, drums; Billy Cox, bass; The Ghetto Fighters, background
vocal on *Freedom*; Buzzy Linhart, vibes on *Drifting*; Stevie Winwood and
Chris Wood, vibes on *Ezy Rider*; Buddy Miles, drums on *Ezy Rider*; Gers,
harp on *My Friend*; Steve Stills and Kenny of the Fugs, background
noises on *My Friend*; Emeretta Marks, background vocal on *In From The
Storm*
  Side One: *Freedom; Drifting; Ezy Rider; Night Bird Flying; My Friend*
  Side Two: *Straight Ahead; Astro Man; Angel; In From The Storm;
  Belly Button Window*

'Rainbow Bridge' (September 1971)
  Reprise K 44159
Produced by Jimi Hendrix, Mitch Mitchell, Eddie Kramer, John Jansen
  Side A: *Dolly Dagger* (Mitch Mitchell, drums; Billy Cox, bass; Ghetto
  Fighters and Jimi, background vocal; recorded Electric Lady, 1/7/70);
  Earth Blues (Mitch Mitchell, drums; Billy Cox, bass; Ronettes, Buddy
  Miles, Jimi, background vocal; recorded Record Plant, 20/1/70); *Pali
  Gap* (Mitch Mitchell, drums; Billy Cox, bass; Juma Edwards, percus-
  sion; recorded Electric Lady, 1/7/70); *Room Full of Mirrors* (Billy Cox,
  bass; Buddy Miles, drums; recorded Record Plant, 17/11/69); *Star
  Spangled Banner* (Jimi, guitars; recorded Record Plant, 18/3/69)
  Side Two: *Look Over Yonder* (Noel Redding, bass; Mitch Mitchell,
  drums; recorded TTG Studios, 22/10/68); *Hear My Train A-Comin'*
  (Mitch Mitchell, drums; Billy Cox, bass; recorded live at Berkeley
  Community Centre by Wally Heider Recording, 30/5/70); *Hey Baby*
  (New Rising Sun) (Mitch Mitchell, drums; Billy Cox, bass; Juma
  Edwards, percussion; recorded Electric Lady, 1/7/70)

'Hendrix in the West' (November 1971)
  Polydor 2302 018
Produced by Eddie Kramer and John Jansen
  Side One: *Johnny B. Goode* (by Chuck Berry); *Lover Man; Blue Suede
  Shoes* (by Carl Perkins) (Mitch Mitchell, drums; Billy Cox, bass;
  recorded live at Berkeley Community Centre by Wally Heider Record-
  ing, 30/5/70); *Voodoo Child* (Mitch Mitchell, drums; Noel Redding,
  bass; recorded live at the San Diego Sports Arena by Wally Heider)

Side Two: *The Queen* (Traditional); *Sgt Pepper's Lonely Hearts Club Band* (Lennon/McCartney) (Mitch Mitchell, drums; Billy Cox, bass; recorded live at the Isle of Wight by Pye Recording, 30/8/70); *Little Wing*; *Red House* (Mitch Mitchell, drums; Noel Redding, bass; recorded live at the San Diego Sports Arena by Wally Heider Recording)

'War Heroes' (1972)
Polydor 2302 020
The Jimi Hendrix Experience
Mitch Mitchell, drums; except as indicated Billy Cox, bass
Side One: *Bleeding Heart*; *Highway Chile* (Noel Redding, bass); *Tax Free* (Redding, bass); *Peter Gunn Catastrophe*; *Stepping Stone*
Side Two: *Midnight* (Redding, bass); *3 Little Bears*; *Beginning*; *Isabella*

'Soundtrack from the film "Jimi Hendrix" '
Reprise K 64017 (2RS-6481)
Side One: *Rock Me Baby*; *Wild Thing*; *Machine Gun I*; *Interviews I*
Side Two: *Johnny B. Goode*; *Hey Joe*; *Purple Haze*; *Like A Rolling Stone*; *Interviews II*
Side Three: *Star Spangled Banner*; *Machine Gun II*; *Hear My Train A-Comin'*; *Interviews III*
Side Four: *Red House*; *In From The Storm*; *Interviews IV*

'The Jimi Hendrix Experience: Backtrack 3'
Track 99 2407 003
The Jimi Hendrix Experience
(Hendrix, Mitchell, Redding)
One side only: *Hey Joe*; *I Don't Live Today*; *Purple Haze*; *Can You See Me*; *The Wind Cries Mary*; *Stone Free*

'The Jimi Hendrix Experience: Backtrack 4'
Track 99 2407 004
The Jimi Hendrix Experience
One side only: *The Burning Of The Midnight Lamp*; *Are You Experienced*; *If Six Was Nine*; *Remember*; *Gypsy Eyes*; *All Along The Watchtower*

'Monterey International Pop Festival—Otis Redding/Jimi Hendrix Experience'
Reprise 2029 (USA)
Atlantic 940 056 (GB)
Produced by Lou Adler and John Phillips. Recorded live by Wally Heider, 16/17/18 6/67
One side only: The Jimi Hendrix Experience
Mitch Mitchell, drums; Noel Redding, bass
Side One: *Like A Rolling Stone* (Bob Dylan); *Rock Me Baby* (B. B. King/Joe Josea); *Can You See Me*; *Wild Thing* (J. Taylor)

'Woodstock'
Cotillion SD-3-500 (USA)

Polydor 2402 003
Recorded live at Woodstock, 17/8/68
The Jimi Hendrix Experience
Mitch Mitchell, drums; Noel Redding, bass
   Three tracks only : *Purple Haze; Star Spangled Banner; Instrumental Improvisation*

'Woodstock II'
   Polydor 2657 003 (GB)
Recorded live at Woodstock, 17/8/68
The Jimi Hendrix Experience
Mitch Mitchell, drums; Noel Redding, bass
   Seven tracks only : *Red House; Instrumental Improvisation; Villanova Junction Blues; Jam Back At The House; Isabella; Getting My Heart Back Together*

'Experience' (Also available as bootleg 'Live at the Albert Hall')
   Ariola 85 087TT (Germany)
   Ember 85 087 (GB)
   (Also Ember NR 5057)
No production credits. Recorded live at the Albert Hall, 18/2/69
The Jimi Hendrix Experience
Mitch Mitchell, drums; Noel Redding, bass
   Side One : *Sunshine Of Your Love* (Opening Jam) (Bruce/Brown/Clapton); *Room Full of Mirrors* (plus Dave Mason, Chris Wood and 'Rocky')
   Side Two : *C Sharp Blues* (also known as *People, People, People* and *Bleeding Heart*); *Smashing Of Amps*

'More Experience'
   Ember
Recorded live at the Albert Hall, 18/2/69
Produced by Mike Jeffries
The Jimi Hendrix Experience
Mitch Mitchell, drums; Noel Redding, bass
   Side One : *Little Ivey* (in fact, this appears to be the *Little Wing* track on 'Hendrix In The West'); *Voodoo Child; Room Full of Mirrors* (a re-mixed version of the track on 'Experience')
   Side Two : *Fire; Purple Haze; Wild Thing; Bleeding Heart* (a re-mixed version of the track on 'Experience')

'Isle Of Wight'
   Polydor 2302 016
Recorded live at the Isle of Wight by Pye Recording
Mitch Mitchell, drums; Billy Cox, bass
   Side One : *Midnight Lightning; Foxy Lady; Lover Man*
   Side Two : *Freedom; All Along The Watchtower* (Bob Dylan); *In From The Storm*

'Isle Of Wight/Atlanta' or 'The First Great Festivals of the Seventies'
Three tracks from the 'Isle Of Wight' only

'Jimi Hendrix At His Best Vol. 1'
Saga 6313 (GB)
Produced by Mike Ephron. Recorded 1964
Side One: *She Went to Bed with My Guitar; Free Thunder; Cave Man Bells*
Side Two: *Strokin' A Lady on Each Hip; Baby Chicken Strut*

'Jimi Hendrix At His Best Vol. 2'
Saga 6314 (GB)
Produced by Mike Ephron. Recorded 1964
Side One: *Down Mean Blues; Feels Good; Fried Cola*
Side Two: *Monday Morning Blues; Jimi is Tender Too; Madagascar*

'Jimi Hendrix At His Best Vol. 3'
Saga 6315 (GB)
Produced by Mike Ephron. Recorded 1964
Side One: *Young Jim; Lift Off*
Side Two: *Swift's Wing; Spiked with Heady Dreams; Giraffe*

2. IMPORTS AVAILABLE FROM USA

'Faces and Places'
Byg 529912

'Hendrix and Little Richard, Friends from the Beginning'
Ala 1972

'Boots'
TLP 9501

3. OFFICIAL COMMERCIAL SINGLES

(a) With the Experience:
Hey Joe / 51st Anniversary
The Wind Cries Mary / Purple Haze
Foxy Lady / Hey Joe
One Rainy Wish / Up From The Skies
Little Wing / Stars That Play With Laughing Sam's Dice
All Along The Watchtower / Burning of the Midnight Lamp
Crosstown Traffic / Gypsy Eyes
All Along The Watchtower / Voodoo Child (Slight Return)

(b) With the Band of Gypsies:
Stepping Stone / Isabella

4. ALBUMS WITH CURTIS KNIGHT

'Get That Feeling' (released November 1967)
  Capitol ST-2894 (USA)
  London SH-8349 (GB)
Produced by Ed Chalpin. Recorded 1965 to 1967
  Side One: *How Would You Feel; Simon Says; Get That Feeling*
  Side Two: *Hush Now; Welcome Home; Gotta Have A New Dress; No Business; Strange Things*

'Strange Things'
  Side One: *Ballad of Jimi; No Business; Future Trip; Gotta Have A New Dress; Hornet's Nest; Don't Accuse Me*
  Side Two: *Strange Things; Flashing; Hush Now; Knock Yourself Out; Happy Birthday*

'Flashing'
  Capitol ST-2894 (USA)
Produced by Ed Chalpin. Recorded in July and August 1965 unless otherwise indicated
  Side One: *Gloomy Monday; Hornet's Nest ('66); Fool For You Baby ('66); Happy Birthday; Flashing*
  Side Two: *Day Tripper; Odd Ball; Love Love; Don't Accuse Me*

'Jimi Hendrix Live in New Jersey'

'The Great Jimi Hendrix in New York' (double)
  Side One: *Hush Now; Love Love; Future Trip; Day Tripper*
  Side Two: *Ballad of Jimi; Simon Says; Level; How Would You Feel*
  Side Three: *Get That Feeling; Happy Birthday; Simon Says; Hornet's Nest*
  Side Four: *No Business; Gotta Have A New Dress; Hush Now; You Don't Want Me*

'The Eternal Fire Of Jimi Hendrix'
  Hallmark SHM 732 (GB)
  Side One: *How Would You Feel; Love Love; Hush Now; Flashing; Day Tripper*
  Side Two: *You Don't Want Me; Hush Now; Simon Says; Level; Love Love*

'Early Jimi Hendrix'

'Early Jimi Hendrix Vol. 2'
  1967 Material

'Get That Feeling / Flashing' (double)

'Jimi Hendrix Live'

'What'd I Say'
  MFP 5278
Produced and recorded by Ed Chalpin
  Side One: *Driving South; California Night*
  Side Two: *On the Killing Floor; What'd I Say; I'll Be Doggone;*
  Bright Lights, Big City

'Birth of Success'
  MFP 50053 (GB)
  Side One: *I'm a Man; Sugar Pie Honey Bunch; Get Out of My Life*
  Woman; Ain't That Peculiar
  Side Two: *Last Night; Satisfaction; Land of a Thousand Dances; UFO*

'Birth of Success
  Hor-Zu SHZE 293 (Germany)
Recorded live at the St George's Club 20, Hackensack, New Jersey
  Side One: *Driving South; I'm A Man; On The Killing Floor*
  Side Two: *California Night; Ain't That Peculiar; What I'd Say;*
  Bright Lights, Big City

'Jimi Hendrix and Curtis Knight'
  London SL 3001/2
New York, 1965

5. OTHER COMMERCIAL RECORDINGS INCLUDE:

'False Start' by Love
Hendrix plays on one track only

'Stephen Stills' by Stephen Stills
  Atlantic 2401004
Hendrix plays on one track, *Old Times Good Times*. The record is
dedicated to James Marshall Hendrix

'In The Beginning Together'
  Buddah T-Neck TNS 3007
Recorded 1964 or 1965. Hendrix plays with the Isley Brothers

'Two Great Experiences Together' with Lonnie Youngblood
  Haple 6004
Another very early recording

'Jimi Hendrix and Lonnie Youngblood'
  Platinum LPM 6004 (GB)
New York, 1965

'You Can Be Anyone This Time Around'
  Douglas I

Hendrix is among the friends playing with Tim Leary

'Jimi Hendrix' (also available as bootleg 'Home At Woodstock'
CSD 1564)
    Saga 6307
    Also on Pantonic PAN 6307
With friends Michael Ephron, Juma Edwards and others
    Side One: *Impromptu No. 1, (Baroque I)*
    Side Two: *Impromptu No. 2, (Baroque II); Impromptu No. 3,*
    Virtuoso (Part 1 Berceuse, Part 2 Flying, Part 3 Perpetuum Mobile)

'The Jimi Hendrix Experience with Ginger Baker'
    Muma Records, California

'Friends and Angels Again' by Martha Velez
    Horizon S-7-63867 (Germany)
Mitchell definitely drums on this record

'McGough & McGear'
    Parlophone 1967
Hendrix plays on some tracks

'Buddy Miles Express'
    Mercury 1968
Hendrix plays on some tracks and he wrote sleeve notes

Hendrix was also producer of 'Sunrise' by Eire Apparent (1969)

6. BOOTLEGS READILY AVAILABLE INCLUDE:

'Broadcasts' (all early Experience 1967-68)
Also titled 'Live Experience 1967-68'. Released in California as 'Good-
bye Jimi' on Kustom Records
    Side One: *Purple Haze; Wild Thing* (live from the Savile Theatre);
    Voodoo Child; Hey Joe; Sunshine Of Your Love (live from the Lulu
    Show, 1968)
    Side Two: *Driving South; Experiencing The Blues; Hound Dog; Little*
    Miss Lover (live from Top Gear); *Love Or Confusion; Foxy Lady; Hey*
    Joe; Stone Free (live from Saturday Club)

'Wow'
Recordings from Woodstock and Monterey festivals
    Monterey: *Like A Rolling Stone; Rock Me Baby; Can You See Me;*
    Wild Thing
    Woodstock: *Red House; Instrumental Interlude; Star Spangled*
    Banner; Villanova Junction Blues

'Skyhigh' (from early 1968)
    Side One: *Red House; Blues Jam*

Side Two : *Bleeding Heart* (jam with Johnny Winter and a drunken Jim Morrison)

'Hendrix Alive' or 'Live In LA'
With Cox and Mitchell (probably from the first half of 1970)
Side One : *Spanish Castle Magic*; *Foxy Lady*; *Getting My Heart Back Together*
Side Two : *Message to Love*; *Ezy Rider*; *Machine Gun*; *Room Full Of Mirrors*
Side Three : *Hey Baby*; *Freedom*
Side Four : *Star Spangled Banner*; *Purple Haze*; *Voodoo Child*

'Maui Hawaii'
Side One : *Hey Baby*; *Red House*
Side Two : *Villanova Junction Blues*; *Hear My Train A-Comin'*

'J.H. Isle Of Wight Vol. 1'
With Cox and Mitchell at the Isle of Wight 1970
Side One : *Lover Man*; *Freedom*; *Red House*
Side Two : *Machine Gun*

'J.H. Isle Of Wight Vol. 2'
Side One : *Foxy Lady*; *Hey Baby*; *Ezy Rider*
Side Two : *Voodoo Child* (Slight Return); *In From The Storm*

7. JUST RELEASED

'Loose ends ...' (1973)
  Polydor 2310 301 Super
Executive producer Michael Jeffries
Remix and produced by Alex Trevor at Electric Ladyland Studios
  Side One : *Coming Down Hard On Me Baby*; *Blue Suede Shoes* (Perkins); *Jam 292*; *The Stars That Play With Laughing Sam's Dice*; *The Drifter's Escape* (Bob Dylan)
  Side Two : *Burning Desire* (*not the same as Fire*); *I'm Your Hoochie Coochie Man* (Willie Dixon); *Have You Ever Been* (*to Electric Ladyland*) (Noel Redding, bass on side 1, track 4 only; Billy Cox, bass; Buddy Miles, drums and background, vocals on side 1, track 2 and side 1, tracks 1 and 2; Mitch Mitchell, drums)

Index

Index